BECAUSE OF BAGHDAD

*What a Father Would Say About Life,
if He Didn't Come Home to Say It*

BART NEWMAN

*May Christ
lead you always!*

Bart Newman

For

Kate, Luke, and all my future children—

your daddy loves you.

Contents

Introduction—*The Hero of the Day*..................... *ix*

Chapter 1   War's Greatest Gift......................17
Chapter 2   Character Under Fire 27
Chapter 3   Six Signs of the Faithful
               Follower 47
Chapter 4   Five Facets of the Lasting
               Leader 65
Chapter 5   Fit for the Fight............................81
Chapter 6   Financially Free............................93
Chapter 7   Making Marriage Matter............113
Chapter 8   What Am I Going to Do
               with My Life? 131
Chapter 9   Your Father's Greatest
               Hope 147

Notes...155
I Want to Hear from You!..............................161

Introduction — *The Hero of the Day*

The day I deployed for Iraq was one of the hardest days of my entire life. It was February 3, 2005, and the weather was unseasonably cold and rainy for Fort Bragg, North Carolina. As I stood in the middle of Boley Field getting wetter each second, a master sergeant barked out names as he completed the final accountability checks. While only halfway listening, my mind turned to my family that I was leaving for a year.

The previous evening I had said goodbye to my eight-month-old baby girl, Kate. That night she was tired and ready for her mommy to nurse her, but I did not want to let her go. I understood what she could not: this would be our last moment together for a very long time. As she squirmed in my lap, I finished reading her favorite story and then kissed her little head. I whispered in her ear that I loved her and always would, and as I handed her to my wife, I left tears in her hair.

It was late that night before Julie and I finally got in bed. But instead of sleeping, we silently held hands and stared at the ceiling. We had known this moment would arrive for several months and yet when it finally came, we were still unprepared. I do not know how long we lay there in silence, but finally, we fell asleep.

We woke a little after 4 a.m. so Julie could drop me off that morning while her mother stayed with our sleeping daughter. Although families were permitted to say goodbye at the airstrip and watch their soldier get on a plane, we decided this would be too difficult with a nursing baby. Instead, we arrived at Fort Bragg early and sat in the back of our minivan holding each other and fighting back tears. At the appointed time, we drove to a secluded place in front of a weeping willow tree—how ironic—and said our final good-byes. As we held each other, I began to pray.

I first thanked the Lord for giving me such a wonderful family. Saying goodbye hurt so much and was proof of how much we loved each other and how blessed we were. I then asked the Lord to protect me in Iraq and help me serve my superiors and subordinates to the best of my ability. Finally, I asked the Lord to take care of my family in my absence. I asked the Lord to use the time we spent away from each other to bring us closer to Him. I asked that the special relationship Julie and I enjoyed since high school would continue to flourish even though we would be separated by such a great distance. We kissed, she got in the minivan, and I watched her drive away as raindrops slipped off the brim of my patrol cap.

The master sergeant was still calling out names when the following thought formed in my mind: *Sometimes everything has to be taken away to understand what is truly important in life.* On that cold rainy morning, I was not thinking of my golf swing, the financial markets, or the latest news out of our nation's capital—all things that might grab my attention on a usual day. Those temporal concerns were nowhere to be found. The only concerns I had were those that had eternal significance—my relationship with the Lord and my young family.

In Baghdad, I served as a Judge Advocate or military lawyer for the Multi-National Corps Iraq (MNC-I). The MNC-I Commander was the commander of all military operations in the country, and my job was to advise the command on numerous legal issues, especially those concerning detention operations and rules of engagement for lethal and non-lethal targeting. As part of my job, I watched daily something called the Commander's Battle Update Assessment (BUA). This briefing took place in a room that resembled a very large movie theater. But instead of reclining seats, desks with computers lined each successive row and tiered upward like a stadium (similar to a NASA command center). At these stations, members of the entire corps staff managed the war.

The purpose of the BUA was to paint a picture of the current state of the war so that the commander could provide the best guidance to the troops. In forty-five minutes, the BUA succinctly described what was going right and wrong in Iraq as it related to the mission. At the end of this presentation, the chaplain would introduce a PowerPoint slide titled "The Hero of the Day." A picture of a recently killed service member would adorn a screen as large as one at a movie theatre. The chaplain would then explain how this hero was killed, describe the family he was leaving behind, and finally read a statement from a family member or the hero's unit. The chaplain would conclude by saying something like, "May God bless Staff Sergeant Jones...may his memory be eternal."

Although I watched this update a few hundred times, I never failed to pause when the chaplain presented the Hero of the Day. While my mind might wander during other parts of the briefing, it was always focused during this time. And I was not alone. The corps staff assembled in that cavernous room grew quiet. The frenetic activity ceased as we looked into the eyes of that hero. In a moment of reverence, we all silently said goodbye.

For some reason, one particular hero really touched me. The soldier had recently been killed on a convoy by a roadside bomb. He was about my age and married with little children. The chaplain read a passage by his grieving wife describing what a wonderful husband and father he had been. Her words were as touching as they were sobering.

Later that evening reclining in my bunk, I began to think again of this soldier and all the ones like him who had died in Iraq and were leaving loving wives and little children. Like me, they left home knowing

Iraq was a dangerous place, but fully expected to return. However, they were not coming home, and now their families would have to make a home without them. Those little children would face a life without a father to instruct them, make them laugh, or hold them when they cry. They lost more than a play-mate, provider, and protector. They lost a daddy.

Before I left for Iraq, my wife gave me a copy of the picture that adorns the cover of this book. It was taken the day I graduated from Airborne School, just a few months before I deployed. As I sat on my bunk and closed my eyes to picture my little girl's face, I began to realize I was no more special than the Hero of the Day. I could just as easily be killed on a convoy or have a random mortar explode near my bunk. If that happened, Kate would be another one of those children growing up without a daddy. I forced myself to imagine what that would mean, and it broke my heart. I would not be there to tell her about heaven and see her develop a relationship with the Lord. I would not be there to help her grow into a young woman and see her graduate from high school. I would not be there to tell her what a real man should be, and then walk her down the aisle to marry him. I would not be there to help her under-stand and navigate all the difficult issues of life that if she failed to address in God's way, would leave her with pain and loss. I would not be there to be her daddy.

As I internalized my grief, God began to put this book on my heart. It started with a journal where I began to write what I would say about life, in case

I did not come home to say it. I wrote about war and how it forced me to face my mortality. I wrote about character and what makes a good leader and follower. I wrote about the importance of physical fitness, managing money, and making a marriage that matters. By the time I returned home, I had seventy-two handwritten pages that basically described how to get the most out of life. To make the book a reality, I would only need to commit to paper the thoughts I conceived in combat.

That being said, I still struggled over the decision to write it. Ten months after returning home, Julie gave birth to our son, Luke. Our family was growing and our lives were getting busier. Writing a book would be an all-consuming task, so much so that I felt I could not begin until I got off active duty. By that time, I would no longer have a job and a monthly pay check. To pay the bills, Julie and I would have to deplete the savings we accumulated the year I was in Iraq.

Despite these concerns, I decided to move forward for three reasons. First, I believed God wanted me to put on paper the words He put on my heart. Second, I wanted to give my children a timeless gift. For when they are adolescents, young adults, or even parents themselves, I want them to pick up this book and hear my love echo through the pages as I tell them everything I would want them to know. Finally, I hoped the book would be beneficial to others. Because Iraq forced me to re-evaluate my life, I gained a unique insight into what is truly important. Only by sharing this perspective could I help others to do the same.

Therefore, given all my successes and failures, I present this handbook to help you get the most out of life. I present a plan to help you live the life that God desires so that eternity is different because of you! I present: *Because of Baghdad.*

Chapter 1

War's Greatest Gift

It is better to go to a house of mourning than to go to a house of feasting, for death is the destiny of every man; the living should take this to heart.

—Ecclesiastes 7:2

You're going to spend more time dead than alive, so you ought to plan for it.

—Zig Ziglar

Going to war is extremely difficult. The warrior is separated from friends and family, and will likely face physical danger. However, this separation and physical danger are more of a gift than we might think. In a very real sense, war presents the warrior with a unique opportunity. For in a foreign land, he is forced to finally face his mortality. No longer is death a notion that can be simply ignored or stored in the recesses of his mind; the carnage of the conflict make this an impossibility. Instead, he must confront that indisputable truth: death is the destiny of every man.

Although this might seem morbid, it is really a gift because we cannot get the most out of this life until we are prepared for our death. Stu Weber learned this as a captain assigned to the Fifth Special Forces Group during Vietnam. In his book *Tender Warrior*, Weber describes facing his mortality and his subsequent awakening with the following:

> My face was pushed into the muddy banks of a small trench at the perimeter of a Special Forces A-Camp. Something was out there...And we were their target...
>
> In some ways, it was almost as bad as being under attack. Just knowing that there were several companies of crack North Vietnamese regulars out there on the perimeter—waiting for the right moment to come screaming out of the forest—turned life into a waking nightmare. There in that muddy ditch—reeling from the fears and threats of imminent combat—I finally heard the wakeup call. I finally faced the real possibility that I would never go home. I finally faced up to the fact that I might not "beat the odds." My life might indeed end in that faraway place. It might not be "someone else" leaving that valley in a body bag. It might not be "someone else" flying home in a silver, flag-draped coffin.

I could actually die. Within hours. Minutes. Seconds. As I grappled with those thoughts, a question burned its way to the surface of my mind. After smoldering in my soul for months, the question now burst into hot flame. What matters? What really matters?[1]

Stu Weber was not your average soldier. He was the best of the best. He was an Airborne Ranger who wore the Green Beret as a member of a Special Forces Group. To earn these distinctions, he had to endure months and months of training which included endless marches, screaming instructors, and days on end with little food or sleep. When he got to Vietnam, he further distinguished himself by winning three Bronze Stars. Stu Weber is a warrior in every sense of that word.

But even a warrior like Weber remembers "reeling from the fears and threats of imminent combat."[2] He remembers facing death on a hillside in Vietnam and how that threat finally woke him from the façade of this world which says we will live forever.

MOMENTS OF CLARITY

Even before I arrived in Iraq, I encountered the same moment of clarity described by Stu Weber. It was during the U.S. Army's Airborne School at Fort Benning, Georgia. As if it were yesterday, I remember standing behind a C-130 in the hot Georgia sun waiting to walk up the plane's back gate. Along with the other aspiring paratroopers, I found myself in one of two single file lines standing under the uncomfortable strain of my parachute harness and weight of my rifle, rucksack, and equipment. The four large propellers were engaged and discharged an exhaust of hot fumes that hit my face, and it felt as though I were standing in front of a large fan. Because of the engine noise and my earplugs, the only thing I could really hear were my own thoughts. *Bart, you're about to jump out of a perfectly good airplane!*

My daughter Kate was just over three months old and the responsibility of parenthood weighed on me. Although I knew it was extremely rare for a paratrooper to be killed on a jump, I also knew that it happened. Our instructors trained us how to deal with equipment malfunctions, airborne collisions, and the other perils of jumping and landing, but it could still be as dangerous as it was exhilarating. Despite all the great training, I still had to face the fact that something could happen to me.

Once in Iraq, I faced this again as I departed on my first convoy mission. Although I had been "outside the wire" several times by helicopter on missions to assess various detainee facilities, I had never traveled the streets of Baghdad. That day we would be leaving Camp Victory and traveling west to the infamous Abu Ghraib prison. It was there, in the early stages of the war, that American soldiers mistreated Iraqi prisoners who were being held. The pictures of soldiers gesturing at nude, hooded Iraqis had streamed across the world via Internet and

TV, and served to erode the moral authority of the American cause.

What most people do not know about Abu Ghraib is that it lies in one of the most hostile areas of Baghdad, a densely Sunni neighborhood that surrounds the prison like the ocean surrounds an exposed island. As such, the prison receives frequent mortar fire. The young soldiers at Abu Ghraib work and sleep under the constant threat of attack, from inside and out.

I remember well the convoy brief before we loaded our weapons and drove out Camp Victory's gates. We formed a semicircle around the convoy commander, and he stated matter-of-factly that we would be driving on the most dangerous streets in Iraq. Soldiers moving up and down these routes are attacked constantly by means of roadside bombs and small arms fire. If we were attacked, we would do the following. If anyone was injured, we would do the following. Then he asked if there were any questions. I took my eyes off the commander, and I looked at the others around me and noted the seriousness of the moment. There were no jokes. There were no smiles. The tension in the morning air was almost tangible.

My final moment of clarity took place a month before we were due to return home. It was the evening of December 10, 2005. I was hanging out with my good friend, Captain Step Nolten. While sitting in his trailer, we began to hear the sound of one of our .50 caliber machine guns firing on a target. Because this was fairly common, we did not think much of it. But instead of stopping, it only seemed to increase. And then it was joined by the echo of other .50 calibers churning out rounds. These machine guns were on towers surrounding the perimeter of Camp Victory, and it sounded as if they were really laying into something. Five minutes later, the noise piqued our curiosity. We decided to go outside and check it out.

I will never forget that sight. The sky was alive with purple and green tracer rounds illuminating the early evening air. The sounds of rifles and automatic machine guns reverberated off every structure. I panned the night sky where tracer rounds covered a 180 degree arc. Suddenly, flares were shot down Route Irish illuminating the highway which connects Camp Victory with the U.S. Embassy in the Green Zone. In all my time in Baghdad, I had never seen our gate guards shoot flares; it seemed they wanted a better view of an advancing threat.

Also standing alongside me were several other soldiers, not saying a word, but all thinking the same thing: the insurgents are trying to attack Camp Victory. Because of its importance as the operational headquarters of the war, Victory was always under threat of attack. But because of its size and the number of troops housed there, we largely dismissed the threat as nothing more than a suicide attempt. Well, it seemed the insurgents might just be making such an attempt that night. And because the gunfire emanated from all sides of our sprawling compound, it seemed the insurgents had orchestrated a dynamic, complex attack.

All of a sudden, I heard the whiz of a bullet pass by and impact within meters of us. Soldiers ducked for cover.

"Nolten," I yelled, "get down!" All six foot four inches of him crouched low, and he took off running. Once we made our way back to his trailer, we grabbed our weapons and hunkered down on the floor. Nolten threw on his body armor and helmet. I looked for his roommate's equipment, but it was nowhere to be found.

As we lay there, my mind began to race. We had been at Camp Victory for almost eleven months, and besides the occasional mortar and rocket fire, insurgents had made no serious attempt to attack Victory in force. It was almost a month before we would return home, and the enemy was trying to attack. Bad guys were coming inside the wire, and it was about to get ugly.

While I waited for what was coming next, my mind automatically shifted to something else. Just like it did at Airborne School and on my convoy to Abu Ghraib, my mind focused on the eternal things of this world—my relationship with the Lord and my little family.

Lying in Nolten's trailer, I said the same prayer that I had said on those prior two occasions: "Lord, please give me your strength so I may do my duty. Shelter me from harm. But if it is your will that I not return home, welcome me into heaven, protect my family in my absence, and compensate them for the loss of a loving husband and daddy."

My thoughts were suddenly interrupted by the loud speakers installed throughout the post. A voice boomed, "Camp Victory, Camp Victory, you are not under attack! Repeat, you are not under attack! Seek cover and remain there." Puzzled, Nolten and I looked at each other. The crack of gunfire still echoed loudly throughout the trailer, and now the voice over the speaker said we were not under attack. It made no sense. A couple of minutes later, the same voice came on again and delivered the same message.

After thirty minutes, we decided to leave the trailer and go up to the palace to find out what was really happening. Once there, we ran into my room-mate Captain Kris Mack.

"Did you see that? Iraq just beat Syria in soccer… all that craziness out there is celebratory gunfire!" Nolten and I let it all sink in and then broke out into laughter.

Even though it ended up being the funniest story of the deployment, the incident definitely had a serious side. Eight people on Camp Victory were injured from the gunfire, including a friend and fellow captain—a bullet grazed the side of his head, and he only missed losing an eye by centimeters. For me, it was another moment of clarity, a reminder that life is fleeting, and it was time to do something with it. I was forced to focus on what mattered most, and what I should be living for.

GET PREPARED

You may never experience events like these which compel you to face your mortality. But because random death is not confined to war zones, you should be prepared to face it anyway. You may suddenly die today in a car wreck or tonight in the middle of your sleep. The truth is we do not know when death is coming, but we know that it will come.

It is said that "there are no atheists in a foxhole." While some might disagree, I identify with this statement completely. For whenever I have faced the possibility of death, I have always cried out to God. And for good reason. Because like most people, I believe we will spend eternity somewhere — that this life is not simply the end of our story. Even if it is unsettling, I believe we should force ourselves to investigate where our story will lead. It is a fundamental principle: We cannot get the most out of life, until we are prepared for our death.

Chapter 2

Character Under Fire

*The character of even a child can be known
by the way he acts—whether what he does is
pure and right.*
                            —Proverbs 20:11 (TLB)

*Good character is more to be praised than
outstanding talent. Most talents are to some
extent a gift. Good character, by contrast,
is not given to us. We have to build it piece
by piece—by thought, choice, courage and
determination.*
                            —John Luther

On November 30, 2005, the *Los Angeles Times*
alleged that U.S. military contractors had paid
Iraqi journalists to plant stories in Iraqi newspapers.
This article was soon followed by similar ones in the
New York Times, *The Washington Post*, and other
major newspapers across the country. The press was

outraged, claiming any such program violated basic standards of journalism. As a result, political leaders in Washington D.C. wanted answers.

Senator John Warner, the Chairman of the Armed Services Committee, said he was "gravely concerned about the situation."[1] Senator Edward Kennedy, a member of the Armed Services Committee, said it was "a devious scheme to place favorable propaganda in Iraqi newspapers."[2] Even President George W. Bush—through his spokesman—was said to be "very concerned."[3]

Although Baghdad is more than six thousand miles from Washington D.C., we heard these allegations immediately. Military leaders from the Pentagon began to pepper us with questions. To get answers, General George Casey, the overall commander in Iraq, tapped Rear Admiral Scott Van Buskirk to conduct an investigation. We only had a few days until the admiral arrived in Baghdad. This was our window of opportunity.

First, we needed to collect all documents relating to the program. We had nothing to hide, and Admiral Van Buskirk was going to get everything we could find. Second, we needed to do everything in our power to protect the Iraqi journalists involved. Unfortunately, some of the initial news reports cited—by name—the newspapers that had printed the articles. Because insurgents target Iraqis that assist coalition forces, the editors of these papers were now in danger. In fact, at least two of them received death threats from insurgents.[4] A massive effort to protect them would be necessary.

All this required a lot of work, and by this time in the deployment, we were tired. We had been working at least seventy hours a week for the last ten months. And this "scandal" only made life more unbearable. As I looked at my peers, superiors, and subordinates, their faces showed the strain.

What was interesting, however, was the way different soldiers handled the situation. Some became almost despondent. All the bravado and arrogance disappeared, only meekness remained. Perhaps some feared the congressional spotlight, knowing that any opportunity for future promotion would dissolve under those scorching lights.

At the same time, however, others rose to the occasion and flourished under the pressure. Our commander, Lieutenant General John R. Vines, was one of them. He said that the accusations of wrong-doing were false, and his team had followed the law. Furthermore no one should worry, because if the media had a problem with the way he was running the war, then he would take the heat. As if channeling President Harry S. Truman, Lt. Gen. Vines made it clear that the buck stopped with him.

Although not in charge of the war, several of my colleagues flourished as well. As the "worker bees" of the corps, they went beyond the call of duty. No matter what kind of crazy request was made, they just put their heads down and got the job done. Their service was absolutely inspiring.

Once the investigation was completed several months later, Lt. Gen. Vines was proven right. His solders had neither broken the law nor violated

Department of Defense regulations.[5] For most, this "scandal" conceived in the Beltway served only to produce sleepless nights in Baghdad. But for me, it produced something far greater. For under the enormous strain of that time, I got a glimpse into the true character of my peers, superiors, and subordinates. On December 4, 2005, I recorded the following in my journal:

> The last few days have been out of this world busy…I finished working on a project last night at 2 a.m. … all these allegations from newspapers back home have had us hopping like crazy. What is interesting is that you really see what someone's character is made of when they are stressed and tired.

The pressure and strain of that experience exposed everyone's character; basically, one either had it, or lacked it. However, it also reminded me that nothing is more important than good character. While it is nice to have superior strength or intelligence, good character is far more valuable. And everyone—from the four star general to the brand-new private, from the corporate CEO to the volunteer at the local church—needs good character.

WHAT IS GOOD CHARACTER?

What does it mean to have good character? Ultimately, having good character means doing what is right. In the Army, someone has good character if they take the hard right, not the easy wrong. Google—one of the most famous and most profitable companies in the world—embraces the same notion, but states it in the negative. Its motto urges: Don't be evil.

The Bible makes a similar statement: "Be careful to do what is right in the eyes of everybody" (Rom. 12:17). Finally, Andy Stanley, the senior pastor of North Point Ministries, provides my favorite definition. He says good character is doing what is right, even when it is hard.

Whether it is from the Army, a leading corporation, the Bible, or even a prominent pastor, the message is the same: *Do What is Right*. Simply put, good character is doing what is right regardless of the consequences. But what does it mean to do what is right? Interestingly, we all seem to know. C.S. Lewis observed that "human beings, all over the earth, have this curious idea that they ought to behave in a certain way, and cannot really get rid of it."[6] This innate sense of right and wrong—the Law of Nature—is the imprint of God on the human soul. During the war against the Nazis, C.S. Lewis explained:

This law was called the Law of Nature because people thought that every one knew it by nature and did not need to be taught it. They did not mean, of course, that you might not find an odd individual here and there who did not know it, just as you find a few people who are colour-blind or have no ear for a tune. But taking the race as a whole, they thought that the human idea of decent behaviour was obvious to every one. And I believe they were right. If they were not, then all the things we said about the war were nonsense. What was the sense in saying the enemy were in the wrong unless Right is a real thing which the Nazis at bottom knew as well as we did and ought to have practiced? If they had had no notion of what we mean by right, then, though we might still have had to fight them, we could no more have blamed them for that than the colour of their hair.[7]

As Lewis so clearly points out, we all ultimately have an inner sense of what is right. The only question is whether we will rise to the challenge, and whether we will choose to do what is right regardless of the consequences.

FIVE CHARACTER TRAITS OF GOOD CHARACTER

Even if we know what is right, I still believe it is helpful to illustrate what doing right looks like. In fact, I have come to believe that doing right manifests itself in five character traits: Humility, Loyalty, Kindness, Honesty, and Courage. While these are not the only traits which produce good character, good character cannot be obtained without them.

Humility

Colonel Ben Hodges is one of the most celebrated soldiers of Operation Iraqi Freedom. At
the war's beginning in 2003, Col. Hodges was the
brigade commander of the 1st Brigade, 101st Airborne
Division. This brigade is known as the "Bastogne
Brigade" for the division's heroics during World
War II at the town of Bastogne, Belgium.

Made famous by Stephen Ambrose's book *Band
of Brothers* and the HBO mini-series by the same
name, this unit was surrounded by as many as fifteen
German divisions during the coldest winter in years.[8]
Despite facing incredible odds, the Americans refused
to surrender. In fact, when the German commander
requested their surrender, Brigadier General Anthony
McAuliffe famously returned the following message:
"NUTS! The American Commander."[9] This German
offensive—the Battle of the Bulge—was Hitler's last
desperate attempt to reverse the course of the war.
Because of the heroism of the men at Bastogne, it
failed.

As Col. Hodges and his aptly named Bastogne
Brigade waited in the deserts of Kuwait for the order
to invade Iraq, a tragedy befell them. One of their
own soldiers, Sergeant Hassan Akbar, attempted to
take out the brigade's leadership by throwing hand
grenades into the command tent. Two officers were
killed and fourteen were injured, including Col.
Hodges. Despite the loss of several key leaders and
his own injuries, Col. Hodges would not be deterred.

He went on to lead the brigade into Iraq and fight some of the war's largest and most decisive battles.

When our unit deployed to Iraq, it was my first tour and Col. Hodges' second. This time, however, he was the Chief of Operations for all coalition forces. Working in Operational Law, I observed Col. Hodges for an entire year and found him to be an amazing man in many ways. What impressed me more than anything was his humility. Of all the men on Camp Victory, not a one had earned the right to walk around like a peacock more than Col. Hodges. He was a war hero, and everyone knew it. But no matter where he went, he smiled at everyone. When subordinates saluted him, he never failed to return the salute with a "Hey, how ya doing?" This might not seem like a big deal, but he probably returned at least fifty salutes just going to the chow hall every day. Over a year, that adds up.

The Bible says, "Do nothing out of selfish ambition or vain conceit, but in humility consider others better than yourselves" (Phil. 2:3). Col. Hodges treated everyone as if they were the more important person. While other senior officers might have strutted with an attitude of self-importance, Col. Hodges walked with an air of humility.

Near the end of the deployment, Lt. Gen.Vines, our commander, asked several of the senior officers to give a one-hour presentation on their experiences in the Army. Col. Hodges was the third officer to lead this presentation, and it was interesting to note how his was different from the others. First, while the other officers had very elaborate and colorful

PowerPoint presentations, Col. Hodges used all black-and-white slides. Second, unlike the others, Col. Hodges spent a good part of the presentation describing his weaknesses, and then sharing his techniques for compensating. Finally, and also unlike everyone else, he spent a great deal of time talking about his failures. Instead of using the presentation as an opportunity to thump his chest, he described his failures so the young officers might learn from his mistakes. Observing the humility of such a prominent man was stunning. In fact, Lt. Gen. Vines had to interrupt him several times just to inform the audience of all the accomplishments Col. Hodges failed to disclose.

One of my good friends in Iraq worked for Col. Hodges, and I asked her once what he was like as a boss. She smiled and gave him a powerful compliment. She said, "Everyone worked their butts off for Col. Hodges because he treated them so well." She said they just thought so much of him that they never wanted to let him down. Col. Hodges will one day be a general officer. But this future general, destined for the Army's highest ranks, still considered others better than himself. Because of this humility, there was not an officer around for which soldiers would work harder.

Humility is rare, and at the same time important. If nothing else, it is the antidote to snobbery—one of the most poisonous human traits. If we will only consider others better than ourselves—no matter how prominent we become—we will develop the humility and good character that God desires.

Loyalty

I once read that if we want to develop good character, then we should emulate the character traits of
people we admire. When I conduct this exercise, I
think of loyalty. While loyalty can take many forms,
I admire the following two the most: 1) not criticizing
others; and 2) defending the absent.

Someone once told me that the tongue is the
strongest muscle in the body. While I was surprised
at its strength, I was well aware of its power. The
Bible says, "Reckless words pierce like a sword, but
the tongue of the wise brings healing" (Prov. 12:18).
Because the tongue is such a powerful instrument for
both good and evil, it must be tamed. In the Bible,
James describes why we must tame the tongue with
the following example, "With the tongue we praise
our Lord and Father, and with it we curse men, who
have been made in God's likeness. Out of the same
mouth come praise and cursing. My brothers, this
should not be" (James 3:9-10).

In Iraq, praise and criticism flowed from my mouth
every day. At any moment, I might earnestly thank
the Lord for my dear family, and then complain about
my co-workers. Regardless of how justified or accu-
rate the criticism might have seemed, it always made
me feel terribly disloyal. While it was sometimes
entertaining to get together with friends and criticize
others, it never accomplished anything worthwhile.
It never changed the individual in question, and it
never made me a better man. After struggling with
this during my year in Iraq, I am convinced that the

following is true: a critical tongue only darkens a spirit that should be the light of the world.

As a result, I am determined not to let a critical word—a word that judges severely—exit my mouth. Instead of criticizing, we should build people up. The Bible says, "Do not let any unwholesome talk come out of your mouths, but only what is helpful for building others up according to their needs, that it may benefit those that listen" (Eph. 4:29). In order to build people up, there may be times when it is necessary to speak words they may not wish to hear. But if these words are spoken in love, they are helpful to our family, friends, and colleagues.

Besides not criticizing others, loyalty also requires us to defend the absent. Dr. Stephen Covey describes this principle in his book, *The 7 Habits of Highly Effective People*. He writes:

> One of the most important ways to manifest integrity is to *be loyal to those who are not present*. In doing so, we build the trust of those who are present. When you defend those who are absent, you retain the trust of those present.[10]

I have often found myself in groups that were unjustifiably criticizing others. Because I disagreed with the criticism, I just smiled and remained silent. Once, a friend of my mine did the most amazing thing—he defended the absent. Instead of following my lead, he interrupted by saying, "You know, you have it all wrong about that guy. He is certainly not perfect, but he is a good fellow."

The reaction to the statement was amazing. Everyone just stared at their feet for a few seconds, probably as ashamed as I was. But the members of that gossiping circle learned something important about my friend. They learned that he was loyal, and as Dr. Covey suggested, he was someone who could be trusted. For me, I admired my friend because he had something I wanted: the loyalty necessary to be a man of good character.

Kindness

A few months before deploying to Iraq, the Army sent me and about fifty other soldiers to Amman, Jordan. The purpose of the trip was to take an Arabic Cultural Awareness Course taught by Jordanian officers. We were housed at a Jordanian Special Forces Camp, and we were there to learn basic Arabic, Iraqi cultural customs, and more about the current fight in Iraq.

On our first day, we assembled in a large auditorium to receive briefings from our Jordanian hosts. The first speaker was the commander of the camp. Right after welcoming us to Jordan, however, he began a long, unprovoked attack on U.S. foreign policy. He said that the war in Iraq was wrong, our support for Israel was criminal, and American people would suffer if there were no change. He took advantage of a captive audience to say something he could only get away with in a foreign land. The room went silent as we stared at this Jordanian with contempt.

As part of the uniform, soldiers have an American flag sewn on their right sleeve—a constant reminder of what they are fighting for. And while no group of soldiers agrees with everything America does, this flag is worn proudly. Simply put, this Jordanian had insulted America in the presence of a group that had sworn to protect it.

Needless to say, the commander's speech generated hostility. Many of my fellow soldiers were ready to leave, and I am sure the Jordanian officers could sense our displeasure. However, instead of leaving, the soldiers went to work. In class after class, they soaked up everything the Jordanians taught. After only a few days, the Americans were speaking functional Arabic with the aid of language cards.

An interesting transformation began to take place. The attitude of the Jordanians slowly changed. They began to laugh with us and share jokes. Somehow they even seemed to grow fond of us. One Jordanian officer even remarked that he was amazed to see so many soldiers walking through camp speaking Arabic and practicing Arabic cultural norms. By the end of the course, many of the Jordanians seemed genuinely sorry to see us leave. They wished us a safe voyage home and even a successful deployment to Iraq.

When I think back to what caused this unexpected transformation, I believe it was chiefly due to kindness. Instead of returning the camp commander's insult with a bad attitude, the soldiers repaid it with kindness. Once the Jordanians realized that the kindness was genuine, they were visibly disarmed.

The Bible simply says, "Be kind and compassionate to one another" (Eph. 4:32). This requirement to be kind is not dependent on whether someone treats us fairly or not. In fact, the Bible says, "Make sure that nobody pays back wrong for wrong, but always try to be kind to each other" (1 Thess. 5:15). The degree to which we live by this principle is one of the truest measures of our character.

Honesty

The Bible says, "Do not steal. Do not lie. Do not deceive one another" (Lev. 19:11). While it is not surprising that God desires honesty from us, it is surprising to what degree he expects it. In sum, uncompromising honesty is the standard, and Jesus makes this clear in the following passage: "Whoever can be trusted with very little can also be trusted with much, and whoever is dishonest with very little will also be dishonest with much" (Luke 16:10).

All of us have been dishonest with little things. We tell "white lies." We borrow from friends and fail to return. We download music off the Internet that we have not paid for. We use the office phone and fax machine for unauthorized purposes. We take office supplies for personal use. We fudge expense reports. We embellish deductions on our tax returns.

While the monetary costs associated with these actions are minimal, Jesus says that the cost to our character is immeasurable. For it is a principle:

"whoever is dishonest with very little will also be dishonest with much" (Luke 16:10). As a missionary during World War II, John Wolfinger was so dedicated to this principal that he was willing to die for it. Andy Stanley—in his book *Like a Rock*—tells Wolfinger's story:

> Wolfinger was leading a group of about one hundred Christian converts in Borneo. When the Japanese military took control of the island, they sought to arrest the missionary and execute him. Wolfinger's followers devised a plan to hide him in the mountains until the danger passed. But Wolfinger reasoned that by running from his captors, he would be giving his new converts the wrong picture of God. When they urged him further, he explained that when the Japanese asked where Wolfinger was hiding, his followers would have to lie, and that was unacceptable. So rather than risk leaving his followers with a compromised picture of God's character, Wolfinger stayed, was captured, and was executed. Wolfinger believed that lying, regardless of the circumstances, did not meet with God's approval. At the expense of his life, he maintained the will to do what was right.[11]

If John Wolfinger was willing to die for this principal, we could at least try to live by it. Instead of excusing and justifying our little dishonesties, we should disavow them. We must recognize that uncompromising honesty is a prerequisite of good character.

Courage

Christmas Eve in Iraq began early. Our office was due to take the Army Physical Fitness Test (APFT), and because we still had work that day, we met before sunrise. Once everyone arrived, we formed up, and then ran out to an unfamiliar part of our sprawling post. We stopped in front of a guard tower and a ten foot stone wall. A few soldiers from our office were waiting there, and it became clear that the APFT was not on the agenda. As it turned out, we were there to learn about Sergeant First Class (SFC) Paul Smith, the first Medal of Honor recipient of Operation Iraqi Freedom. On the very ground on which we stood, SFC Smith had fought to his death. The following excerpt from the Army Field Manual 6-22 tells his story:

> When SFC Paul Smith started his day at the Baghdad Airport on 4 April 2003, he was focused on building a holding pen for enemy prisoners. Before the day was over, he had given his life and saved as many as 100 others in the process.
> SFC Smith was a combat engineer assigned to Bravo Company, 11th Engineer Battalion in support of Task Force 2-7 Infantry. Smith, whose call sign was "Sapper

7," was well liked by his Soldiers. He was a taskmaster and his experience in Desert Storm taught him to train tirelessly and to standard. He was the acting platoon leader when 50-100 of Saddam's well-trained Republican Guard attacked him and his men.

Three of his Soldiers were seriously wounded and Smith helped evacuate them to a nearby aid station that was also threatened by the attackers. He organized a hasty defense. He told one of his Soldiers "we are in a world of hurt."

Selflessly, Smith took over a .50 caliber machine gun in an exposed position. He fired over 300 rounds at the enemy before his gun fell silent. SFC Smith was the only member of his unit to die that day.[12]

The guard tower and stone wall still show signs of the heroic battle. The surfaces are riddled with bullet holes. The tower is charred in places from a fire or explosion. And as I stood where SFC Smith fought, I tried to imagine the battlefield on that day. The Republican Guard—Saddam's best troops—had an open line of fire. There were no geographic structures to provide cover other than the adjacent stone wall. However, if Smith had retreated there, he could not have fired on the enemy; there would have been no way to counter the advancing threat. His unit was simply exposed. So he stood his ground and defended his men. Only while standing there and contemplating his sacrifice that Christmas Eve morning could I fully grasp his courage.

For most of us, life will never demand such physical courage. Other than confronting the school-yard bully, we will likely never have to summon such inner strength. We have a different challenge. Every day, we must find within us the moral courage to do what is right regardless of the cost. While this courage does not usually earn medals, I believe it does earn the favor of our Lord and the respect of our peers. This became clear to me during a mission to Camp Bucca.

While Baghdad lies between the two rivers in the center of Iraq, Camp Bucca is in the far south of the country, only a few miles from Kuwait's northern border and Iran's southwestern border. To get to Camp Bucca, we flew in a British C-130 to Basra, and then linked up with the Texas National Guard which drove us another hour to the massive detention center. During the convoy, it seemed as if the only structures that interrupted the monotonous desert were oil rigs and the road on which we were trav-eling. We were literally in the middle of nowhere, a stark contrast from Baghdad's densely crowded streets.

I traveled with two other military lawyers, and our mission was to conduct several tribunals under the provisions of Article Five of the Geneva Convention Relative to the Treatment of Prisoners of War (Article 5 Tribunals). These tribunals serve to determine: 1) whether an individual detained on the battlefield committed a belligerent act (i.e., bearing arms against or engaging in other conduct hostile to coalition forces); and if so, 2) whether the individual should receive status as an Enemy Prisoner of War.[13] The first decision had an immediate consequence—if it was determined that the detainee did not commit a belligerent act, he was to be released.

Although captured in Iraq, the detainees in question were from elsewhere. Some came from Palestine, others from North Africa, and still others from Iran and the neighboring Arab states. Each claimed they had come to Iraq for innocent reasons: to attend university, to seek political asylum, or to provide humanitarian aid. We feared, however, that they entered Iraq for another reason: to kill coalition troops. Osama bin Laden called on the Muslim faithful to join their brothers in Iraq and expel the infidel. Many had answered this call. Foreign fighters were responsible for a large percentage of the attacks against American troops and innocent Iraqis. Consequently, this was a threat to be taken seriously.

However as we heard each case, there was often little evidence at our disposal. And in a couple of cases, the only evidence we had matched the testimony of the detainees. At this point we faced a dilemma. Would we decide the case on the merits as we had sworn to do, or would we allow our well-founded suspicions to unfairly bias our decision? Ultimately, would we find the moral courage to abide by our oath—regardless of the consequences?

Later, I realized that this dilemma was really a test of character. I am thankful that we mustered the moral courage to do what was right regardless of the cost. But we did so with a heavy heart. My friend on the tribunal remarked, "I will have nightmares over letting these two guys go." It was horrifying to think that our hands would free those who might leave the detention facility, only to kill Americans. But we took an oath before God to decide each case solely on its merits; now we just needed to find the courage to trust Him to take care of the consequences.

We all must find this courage. We must find the courage to confront friends about destructive behavior, even at the risk of losing the friendship. As a student, we must find the courage to stand up to teachers that demean our faith, even at the risk of a bad grade. As a political leader, we must find the courage to vote our conscience, even at the risk of losing the next election. For once we find this courage, we will become what God desires—people of good character.

Chapter 3

Six Signs of the Faithful Follower

Whatever you do, work at it with all your heart, as working for the Lord, not for men, since you know that you will receive an inheritance from the Lord as a reward. It is the Lord Christ you are serving.

— Colossians 3: 23-24

What makes a good follower? The single most important characteristic may well be a willingness to tell the truth. In a world of growing complexity leaders are increasingly dependent on their subordinates for good information, whether the leaders want to hear it or not. Followers who tell the truth and leaders who listen to it are an unbeatable combination.

— Warren G. Bennis

The soldiers of the Hawaii National Guard were some of the greatest followers in Iraq. To give you an idea of how amazing these soldiers were, it is first necessary to describe the Al Faw Palace, the building they guarded. Saddam Hussein built this enormous palace to commemorate his 1988 victory over the Iranians at the Al Faw Peninsula located in southeastern Iraq. Despite the fact that it was built after the 1991 Gulf War and the imposition of economic sanctions by the United Nations, Hussein spared no expense. In fact, he went so far as to divert water from the Tigris River to create several interconnected man-made lakes on the property. In the middle of the largest of these lakes lies the Al Faw Palace. A long bridge provides the only access to this large stone structure. Once inside, Italian marble covers almost every surface, gold plating is found in every bathroom, and ornate chandeliers hang from twenty-five foot ceilings. This is in addition to the sprawling octagonal-shaped rotunda that is large enough to enclose a small three-story home. From the palace's third-floor patios, one can look down on the Roman-style villas that line the lake's shores and then up to the horizon for a view of the Baghdad skyline. I have been to the White House, the Palace of Versailles, and several other famous residences of the world. Not one is more impressive than the Al Faw Palace.

That being said, the soldiers of the Hawaii National Guard largely did not work inside this beautiful structure. They worked outside, guarding it. To grasp why this is important, it is necessary to understand something about Baghdad's climate. For example, from May until November, there is no rain. That summer, the temperature daily rose above 110 degrees Fahrenheit without the presence of a single cloud to provide shade. These men not only had to stand guard during this weather, but they did it in full "battle rattle"—that is, rifle, helmet, and body armor. The gear alone weighs more than forty pounds, and unfortunately traps body heat. Because their job required them to verify each entrant's identification, they spent most of the day on their feet and as a group, maintained this vigil twenty-four hours a day, seven days a week. If there was a more monotonous and physically exhausting job in Iraq, I am unaware of it.

However, the faces and body language of these men never revealed any discontent. These soldiers— many of whom had never been out of Hawaii—were not disgruntled, but instead displayed the best attitudes on post. Month after month they would greet you with a "Good Day, Sir" and a smile. While the soldiers walking past them were going to work in an air-conditioned office in one of the world's most impressive residences, they never complained, never grumbled, and never failed to do their job to absolute standard.

In our society, we love to celebrate great leaders. We even dissect their lives in hopes of learning their secrets so we might follow in their footsteps. In fact, if you go to any bookstore, the shelves are overflowing with books that promise to tell you how to become that great leader. We all want to be someone that people choose to follow because it satisfies a basic need of our human nature: the need to be significant.

However, if you go back to the same bookstore, how many titles will you find promising to make you the greatest follower? How many books will describe how to serve like the men of the Hawaii National Guard? Ironically, at the large bookstore near my house, the only book I found that examines the role of the follower was located in the leadership section!

Yet, we will be followers more often in life than leaders. For example, try to think of someone who does not have a boss. Even if we became the Chief Executive Officer (CEO) of a large public company—the very top of the corporate ladder—we would have to answer to the company's board of directors. And those directors still have to report to their share-holders. Without exception, we all have to answer to someone. There is always someone appointed over us that we must serve.

Even if we are not that interested in becoming a great follower, God is. And even if the bookstore does not have anything describing the secrets of a great follower, the Bible does. In fact, the Bible says something that is really shocking about this subject: our attitude and performance at work directly reflects our relationship with God. The Bible says, "Whatever you do, work at it with all your heart, as working for the Lord, not for men, since you know that you will receive an inheritance from the Lord as a reward. It is the Lord Christ you are serving" (Col. 3:23-34).

When we are at work, we are not really working for the boss; we are working for the Lord. We are, in fact, serving Christ. No matter how unsatisfying our job might be or unreasonable our boss might seem, we are serving Christ when at work.

I believe we should celebrate great followers as much as great leaders because following is often more difficult. It is more difficult because great leaders receive recognition from the world, their peer group, and their subordinates. They are told constantly that they are significant. On the other hand, great followers rarely receive this kind of validation. The world rarely lines up to celebrate them. But even if the world does not celebrate such humble service, God does and is glorified by it. The individual who is motivated by bringing glory to God is the one truly worthy of study, for this is that rare person who basks in the praise of the Lord, instead of men.

THE PORT-O-JOHN GUY

I have had the good fortune to learn from Andy Stanley, the senior pastor of North Point Ministries based in Alpharetta, Georgia. Several years ago, Andy was building a new house, and his good friend Bob was doing the work. One day while pouring the cement for the new driveway, Bob and his construction crew came across an amazing man. At church one Sunday, Andy told the following story about him:

> So Bob was out there pouring our driveway with his crew, and they're out there

scraping and doing the whole deal. All of a sudden he hears this loud music coming from down the street and as he looks up, he sees it's coming from the Port-O-John guy. That's not the official title, but the Port-O-John guy shows up at work sites and cleans the portable toilets. Now if you've ever been around a Port-O-John when it is being cleaned, it is about the most unpleasant thing in the world …well, other than being in one when it's getting cleaned! But anyway, it's awful. So he looks up and here comes the Port-O-John guy. Bob then scans the work site and notices that the Port-O-John is sitting right beside the driveway. All at once, it seemed that the whole crew looked up, noticed the same thing, and just kind of gasped.

The Port-O-John guy gets out of the truck, and the first thing Bob notices is that it's some new guy, not the one who usually cleans the Port-O-John. He's big, got a bunch of tattoos, and is kind of scruffy looking. Well, the guy grabs his tools, his big ol' hose, and then marches up the yard and goes in the Port-O-John. All the crew is just paralyzed waiting for the terrible stench.

Waiting there, Bob begins to realize that the guy has been in there forever. He wonders how long does it really take to clean a 2 ½ by 2 ½ foot space. The guy is making all sorts of noise with his tools bumping around and such. Anyway, he's just taking forever.

Then, all of a sudden, Bob said there was this incredible aroma that came out and went through the air over the whole work site. The crew kind of looked at each other and sniffed. It was the most pleasant odor, and they were kind of shocked.

Well the guy finally comes out and Bob just felt like he had to say something and offered, "You've got that thing smelling so good, kind of makes me want to go in there!"

The Port-O-John guy turns and says in a deep southern drawl, "You know, the guy that's been servicing you has been doing a terrible job, but I'm going to take care of you...it's going to be different from now on out."

Bob paused and said, "Well...thanks."

The guy replies, "I work for the Lord."

Bob muttered, "Uhhh...excuse me..."

And the guy repeats, "I do my work for the Lord." He then picked up his tools, walked down the driveway, and drove back up the street with his music blaring again.[1]

There are a lot of undesirable jobs in this world. Few kids dream of one day being a janitor, garbage man, or even the guy who cleans the Port-O-John. Regardless of how much it actually pays, it certainly does not impress friends at the yearly Christmas party. However, any job done with all one's heart is honorable work. Do not let the tattoos and rough

appearance fool you. The Port-O-John guy understands something that those in high status jobs often
miss: our jobs are not intended to bring us glory; they
are intended to bring glory to God.

Can there be any doubt that the Port-O-John guy
brings glory to God? The way he meticulously and
thoroughly cleaned one of the dirtiest surfaces on
earth provides a unique insight into his relationship
with the Lord. That relationship was so powerful that
he publicly embraced his role as a servant. He did not
try to conceal his identity and the fact that he cleaned
Port-O-Johns—something I might have done in fear
of encountering someone I knew. Instead, he arrived
at the job site with music blaring and tools flying.
He was not embarrassed, because he knows that God
does not care what job we do, as long as we do it with
all our hearts.

SIX SIGNS OF THE FAITHFUL FOLLOWER

The Port-O-John guy is what I call a Faithful
Follower—someone who is willing to work for his
boss on earth as if working for his Father in heaven.
The truth is that God has not asked that much of us.
Few can claim to work under conditions similar to
that of the Port-O-John guy. In fact, most of us work
in very comfortable settings. Recognizing this, we
should be all the more willing to work with all our
hearts as if working for the Lord. If the Port-O-John
guy can do it, so can we.

Once we make that decision, however, we should
ask the following question: How is this ethic practi-

cally manifested in the work place? In other words, what does it mean to really be a faithful follower of our boss, and the Lord? In seeking answers to these questions, I have identified six signs that typify this ideal. I call them the Six Signs of the Faithful Follower.

Faithful Followers Win the Leader's Respect

The Bible makes an interesting statement about how we are to work and live our daily lives.

Make it your ambition to lead a quiet life, to mind your own business and to work with your hands, just as we told you, so that your daily life may win the respect of outsiders and so that you will not be dependent on anybody (1 Thess. 4:11-12).

Our work should win the respect of those we serve. It is not necessary for our leaders to like us (although there is nothing wrong with that), but our conduct in the work place should win their respect. The dictionary defines respect as a feeling of appreciation and regard. We win this feeling of appreciation and regard from our leaders like we win anything else, through concentrated effort over a period of time. Specifically, I have found that this concentrated effort needs to manifest itself in the following three ways.

First, start early. Getting to work before the workday begins will set the tone for the day. It is so easy for us to show up for our job a little late, grab a cup of coffee, and then chat with co-workers for a few minutes. After a time, we finally sit down at our desk, check our e-mail, and then skim the news. However, by the time we actually do any real work, we have lost half the morning. This does not earn the respect of our leaders. Get to work early and start on time.

Second, work hard. The Bible says, "Whatever your hand finds to do, do it with all your might" (Eccl. 9-11). We should give our absolute best so that nothing but excellence is associated with our work. If we do this over a period of time, nothing but excellence will be associated with our names.

Third, keep promises. The Bible says, "When a man makes a vow to the Lord or takes an oath to obligate himself by a pledge, he must not break his word but must do everything he said" (Num. 30:2). We must do what we said we would do, when we said we would do it. If there is a deadline, we meet it. If we promised to call someone, we call them. We must be people who keep our word. This more than anything will allow our leaders to rely on us.

Faithful Followers Give Candid Counsel

At only twenty years old, Warren G. Bennis was the youngest infantry commander fighting in Germany during World War II. For his service, he received the Bronze Star and Purple Heart. After the war, Bennis would go on to be a university president, an author of twenty-seven books, and one of the world's foremost experts on the subject of leadership. However, it is a comment he made about how to be a follower that bears consideration in this context.

> What makes a good follower? The single most important characteristic may well be a willingness to tell the truth. In a world of growing complexity leaders are increasingly dependent on their subordinates for good information, whether the leaders want to hear it or not. Followers who tell the truth and leaders who listen to it are an unbeatable combination.

As an Army lawyer, my job was to advise commanders. This calling required me to be the honest broker, to look at things as they are instead of how we might wish them to be. I have come to believe that regardless of our job titles, we all have this responsibility. If we are going to serve our leaders as we would the Lord, we need to have the courage to tell them what we really think. I say "courage" because often our views might conflict with those of the leader. And because leaders often carry significant authority and control over future advancement, we are tempted to remain silent or simply conform our views to those we know the leader holds.

For example, during various staff meetings in Iraq, I was often amazed by the difference in the tenor of the discussion depending on who was there. When a certain leader was absent, there was a strong debate with various opinions expressed. When this leader was present, however, sometimes it seemed certain persons would simply praise the leader's preferred course of action. While we are all guilty of this from time to time, we must recognize the danger in doing so. First, this kind of speech is flattery. It is motivated out of a selfish desire to procure an advantage (i.e., make the boss like us) and is not a reflection of our sincere beliefs. The Bible says, "A lying tongue hates those it hurts, and a flattering mouth works ruin" (Prov. 26-28). The ruin in this case is that the flattery can lead to poor decisions. Leaders are humans, and it is the reality of our nature that we like to hear how wonderful we are. When subordinates praise our views or join in our critiques, it makes us feel important. We are drawn to the people who flatter our egos, and it is a very uncommon person that can resist this urge. For this reason, flattery is particularly dangerous in an organization because it can influence the leader to make the wrong decision. Flattery robs the leader of our candid advice and by so doing, the chance to make the most informed and best decision.

This calling to give candid counsel extends beyond the decision-making arena. I believe we also owe it to our leaders to tell them if there is a major problem in the organization. For example, my staff section in Iraq suffered at times from poor morale. To a large degree, this was predictable. We were far away from home. We worked six to seven days a week and usually twelve to fifteen hours a day. We were around each other constantly, and unlike back in the States, there was no escape. As such, the minor, inconsiderate things we all do to each other became more intense.

As one might expect, the leadership sometimes made decisions that annoyed their followers. Because we were neither consulted nor given an explanation for the decision, we felt the leadership really did not care. As a result, we grumbled constantly among ourselves and described the shortcomings of those we served. For the most part, however, we never discussed the nature of the problem with those who could actually do something about it—the leaders themselves. It was just easier to complain behind their backs.

We owe our leaders more than that. The Bible makes it clear, "Don't grumble against each other, brothers, or you will be judged" (James 5:9). If there is a major problem in an organization, I believe we owe it to our leaders to voice it. As faithful followers, we owe them the opportunity to address a problem that they probably do not even know exists.

For me, I finally decided to tell the leadership about the poor morale and what policies were responsible for it. I did this not out of courage really, but because I was just sick of my own double-mindedness. I was literally tired of complaining among my co-workers instead of addressing the issue with the proponent of the policy. After requesting an audience with one of the leaders, I described the problem. Unfortunately, he did not agree. He told me he did not have to explain himself, and that I needed to drive on. While my talk did not produce the desired result, it did provide me with a sense of relief. The decision to make a change belonged to my leader. My job was only to give my candid assessment and present the leader an opportunity to fix it. By sharing my views, I faithfully served him, even though he disagreed.

Faithful Followers Propose Helpful Solutions

It is not enough to describe the problem; we must propose a helpful solution. My last boss in the Army was famous for requiring this of his soldiers. If we ever brought up a problem or concern, he would turn and simply ask, "What is your solution?" What I found is that it is much more difficult to design a solution than describe a problem. Anyone can be a critic, but a faithful follower gives their leader something more: a positive way forward.

For example, if there is a problem in our organization, we might say something like this, "Sir, I want you to know that I'm going to do whatever you want, but I have a concern with a policy that is in place. In my opinion, this policy exposes our organization to risk in the following ways. However, if we were to implement this alternative policy, I believe we would mitigate the risk and produce more consistent results."

By following such a course, we have done a number of things. First, we have told the leader that we recognize his authority and are willing to carry out whatever plan he prefers. This humility shows the leader that we recognize our role and want only the best for the organization. Second, we have described the problem. As is often the case, the leader might not even be aware that there is a problem. Third, we have provided a solution, a plan to correct the problem and move the organization forward. Thus in one concise statement, we have fulfilled our role as a faithful follower because we not only described the problem, we presented a positive solution.

Faithful Followers Salute and Execute

When given an order in the military, one simply salutes and executes. The salute symbolizes respect for authority and willingness to abide by the order given. This concept might seem foreign to those not accustomed to military life, but it should not. The truth is that we are all under authority, and God established it. The Bible says, "Everyone must submit himself to the governing authorities, for there is no authority except that which God has established. The authorities that exist have been established by God. Consequently, he who rebels against the authority is rebelling against what God has instituted, and those who do so will bring judgment on themselves" (Rom. 13:1-2).

After giving honest advice, God says to execute whatever decision the leader makes, given that decision is not immoral or violates a tenet of our faith. We owe our leaders absolute allegiance. Sometimes the leader will follow our advice and other times he may not. In fact, sometimes the leader might even ridicule our idea in front of our colleagues. The faithful follower, however, will seek to execute the leader's wishes with as much enthusiasm as if the leader had endorsed his idea. That is the definition of working at something with your whole heart as if working for the Lord.

Instead, we often try to frustrate the leader's decision because he rejected us. Because our egos are hurt by the criticism, we either withhold our best efforts or even defiantly seek to undermine the leader's policy. We may even go a step further and attempt to breed dissension behind the leader's back hoping others will agree that the leader is wrong and we are right. This is selfishness and only makes the organization ineffective and inefficient. The Bible says, "A perverse man stirs up dissension, and a gossip separates close friends" (Prov. 16:28). We must fight our offended egos and refrain from stirring dissension as the perverse do. We must serve our leader as if we are serving Christ. Once a decision is made, salute and execute.

Faithful Followers Share with the Team

Sometimes in organizations there is competition among followers for the leader's favor. The followers believe that if they impress the boss, they will then set themselves up for preferential treatment and future advancement. Because knowledge is such a powerful tool, there is an incentive to withhold this resource in fear of losing an advantage. However, if we succumb to this temptation, we are indicting our own character. We are saying that it is more important for us to do well in front of the boss than for the organization to operate at its optimum efficiency.

Whether we intend to or not, we are actually saying that we are more important than the organization.

While this behavior might help us stand out among our peers, it certainly does not earn favor with God. The Bible says, "One man gives freely, yet gains even more; another withholds unduly, but comes to poverty. A generous man will prosper; he who refreshes others will himself be refreshed" (Prov. 11:24-25). If we are going to serve the Lord by our conduct at work, we cannot withhold unduly from our peers. Instead, we must share freely. We must trust the Lord to secure our future advancement as opposed to relying on our own self-serving conduct.

In addition to sharing critical information, we should also share praise. If we do good work, our names will be associated with projects that are successful. Oftentimes, the leader will come to us to extend his appreciation for what was accomplished. At this point, we face a dilemma: we can either share the praise—and point out the degree to which others made the project a success—or simply accept the praise in silence. It is easy to accept the praise in silence and leave the leader with the impression that we alone are responsible for the favorable result. This is deceptive. Instead, I believe God says to us, "Share with the team and let me worry about your glory."

Faithful Followers Encourage Both Leaders and Followers

There is too much negativity in this world. It impedes our performance and darkens our lives. We can either choose to be a part of the negativity or fight against it. The Bible says to "encourage one another" (1 Thess. 5:11). Through love-inspired enthusiasm, we should encourage both our leaders and fellow followers to be more than they think they can be. We should help them to become what God wants them to be. Invest in others, shine a light on a dark world, and we will become a faithful follower of our leader on earth, and in heaven.

Chapter 4

Five Facets of the Lasting Leader

Sitting down, Jesus called the Twelve and said, "If anyone wants to be first, he must be the very last, and the servant of all."
— Mark 9:35

The first responsibility of a leader is to define reality. The last is to say thank you. In between, the leader is a servant.
— Max DePree

During my first year of law school, I received a Rotary Ambassadorial Scholarship to study at the University of St. Andrews in Scotland. Because my dean allowed me to take the following year off, Julie and I got married right after first year exams and embarked on our voyage across the Atlantic.

As one might imagine, this was an extremely exciting time. First, I could think of no better way to spend my first year of marriage than living in a charming little town on the North Sea of Scotland. Julie and I lived in a one-bedroom apartment only fifty meters off the beach. We did not have a car or television, which gave us plenty of time to bond during long walks as husband and wife. That experience alone would have made that year the best of my life.

However, that was not all. St. Andrews also provided a unique opportunity to learn in a historic place. Founded in 1413, the University of St. Andrews is Scotland's first university and third oldest in the United Kingdom. Furthermore, bordering the school lies the oldest and most famous golf course in the world—the Old Course. For the equivalent of $150, I was permitted to play the Old Course and the four other courses in St. Andrews as many times as I wanted for an entire year.

If that was not enough, I was particularly excited about my course of study. A large part of my master's curriculum centered on business management and strategy—the study of how organizations perform and adapt to a changing business environment. Through case studies, I learned how business leaders inspire their team and position their organizations to succeed.

This subject was of particular interest to me because I knew firsthand how difficult leading can be. During my sophomore year of college, I was elected president of the University of Georgia's

Student Government Association. In this position, I first learned that having a position of authority does not make one a leader. I guess I had hoped that the faculty and my fellow students would adopt my vision because of the position I held. However, this was just not the case. For that reason, I had to constantly ask myself, "How can I do a better job of leading this organization?"

During my tenure as president I had to learn a lot of lessons the hard way. But because leading was so difficult, my interest in the subject was awakened. I realized that if I were ever to become a good leader, I had a lot to learn. So I became an informal student of the subject. I never took a class on leadership, but I took time to get to know the leaders I encountered. I worked to understand what made them great and made others so eager to follow them.

This is to say that my coursework at the University of St. Andrews was going to give me a more disciplined approach to leadership, especially in the business context. And I was not disappointed. Through my professors and classmates—who hailed from almost every continent on the globe—I received an international perspective on leadership that greatly enriched my understanding.

However, it was an unexpected and tragic event that would enable me to learn more about leadership after leaving St. Andrews. After completing my degree, I returned home just prior to the terrorist attacks of September 11, 2001. Watching the towers fall and America's heroic response inspired me to national service. Like many people during that time, I became determined to do what I could to help. While service in the armed forces had always interested me, 9/11 was the event that solidified my intent. If the military would take me, I would join.

While my intent to join the military was not based on a desire to learn more about leadership, the military became my greatest teacher. In fact, my views on leadership were immeasurably shaped by my time in the Army and my year in Iraq. By watching so many of the country's most decorated leaders command under intense pressure, I found what leadership could and should be.

American taxpayers spend a great deal of money educating and training the men and women that lead our military, and for good reason. America has the strongest military in the world, and our citizens must entrust only our very best to direct this awesome force. As such, I view the education I received during my year on the corps staff as the equivalent of an Executive MBA. By just listening and working alongside these distinguished individuals, I learned what no classroom could have ever taught me.

A LEADER IS SOMEONE PEOPLE CHOOSE TO FOLLOW

Based on my year in Iraq and my previous years of study, I have come to believe that a leader is simply someone people choose to follow. By this definition, a leader is not necessarily someone in a position of authority. In fact, I imagine we all know people who hold positions of authority, but have no willing followers.

Like the other services, the Army is very interested in leadership. It has even devoted an entire Field Manual to the subject which defines the soldier leader as:

> An Army leader is anyone who by virtue of assumed role or assigned responsibility inspires and influences people to accomplish organizational goals. Army leaders motivate people both inside and outside the chain of command to pursue actions, focus thinking, and shape decisions for the greater good of the organization.[1]

Even by the Army's definition, holding a position of authority does not make one a leader. Instead, a soldier must inspire and influence others to be a leader. What is really interesting about this definition is that the Army—of all organizations—could have easily associated leadership with position alone. Unlike civilian life, soldiers face imprisonment if they do not follow the lawful orders of their superiors. It really is that simple. The fact that the Army chose not to make this association is important. It shows that even in the Army each person must earn the title of leader. It cannot be ordered, ordained, or decreed; it must be earned.

That being said, the world needs leaders. It needs people who are going to stand up, do what is right, and influence others to do the same. The corporate scandals that led to the downfall of companies like Enron are at their heart, leadership failures. Because this subject is so important, I offer the following observations on leadership which I call the Five Facets of the Lasting Leader. By adhering to these principles, not only will we become a leader, but a leader that stands the test of time. People will choose to follow us not for just a brief moment, but for life.

Lasting Leaders Deny Themselves Privilege

In every organization, there are missions that no one wants. There are hardships that must be endured and obstacles that must be surmounted. But not all of these hardships and obstacles are big. In fact, most are just small inconveniences, but a leader's willingness to share in such things matters. I saw no one understand this principle better than Brigadier General Daniel Bolger.

To travel from Fort Bragg to Kuwait, my unit chartered a commercial airliner. On my flight were several senior officers, the highest ranking being Brig. Gen. Bolger. Like most commercial airliners, our plane had a number of first class seats which were assigned to the highest ranking individuals on the flight. As I took my seat in the back of the plane squished between other soldiers, I saw the very tall frame of Brig. Gen. Bolger coming towards us. I watched curiously to see where he was going, and I noticed that he took a seat right in the middle of coach. While less senior soldiers were sitting in first class, Brig. Gen. Bolger was sitting in the back with his troops, and he stayed there for the duration of the twenty-hour journey.

When we landed in Kuwait, it became even clearer that he intended to stay with his troops. A master sergeant came to the back of the plane and said to him, "Ahh Sir, some people on the ground want you at the front of the plane." Brig. Gen. Bolger countered, "What do they want?" The master sergeant shrugged and replied, "Ahh...I don't know sir...they just want you..." Brig. Gen. Bolger sighed and then said, "Well, it better be a general officer!" As he walked to the front of the plane, he left an impression on the soldiers in the back—*I am not special.*

Once on the ground in Iraq, Bolger continued to deny the privilege due his rank. For example, almost every soldier in Iraq is issued an M-16 rifle. While you want this weapon when going "outside the wire," it is not the preferred weapon on base. For day-to-day living, soldiers prefer the M-9 pistol because it is smaller and lighter. While this may not seem like such a big deal, try carrying an M-16 everywhere you go for a year. On the other hand, it is much easier to carry an M-9 in the comfort of a shoulder holster. The M-9s, however, were reserved mostly for officers of the rank of major and above.

Just like he sat in coach, Brig. Gen. Bolger carried an M-16. No matter where he went or what he was doing, he lugged around the same weapon the rest of the men carried. He understood that sometimes in life the little things make the biggest impression. When leaders deny themselves the privilege of their position, it endears them to their subordinates.

The subordinates say, "This guy doesn't ask me to do anything that he's not willing to do himself." These measures create a reservoir of goodwill which leaders can then tap when they really need it. That is why lasting leaders deny themselves privilege.

Lasting Leaders Take Care of Their People

During college, I once attended a week-long leadership retreat where one of the keynote speakers was Len Sapera, a retired captain in the U.S. Navy. During a discussion, he shared what he considered to be the chief requirement of a leader. Sapera said, "Leaders must take care of their people. Because if you take care of your people, they'll go through walls for you." Sapera described a fundamental principle of human nature: people do not care what you know, until they know that you care.

The Army says that an officer is supposed to be "the first out of the foxhole, and the last to chow." This saying is just an illustration of a truth Jesus shared with his followers, "If anyone wants to be first, he must be the very last, and the servant of all" (Mark 9:35). Lasting leaders have to be the servants of their subordinates. As strange and counter to traditional thought as this might be, it is only this arrangement that will enable true organizational success. Lasting leaders make the following deal with their subordinates—give me your very best, and I will look out for you. I will serve you and take care of you.

When I was in college, a man by the name of Carl E. Swearingen served as president of my university's alumni association. He was better known in the community as the vice president of Bell South—at the time, one of America's largest telephone companies. Because I was a member of an organization that served the alumni association, he would often come and speak to us. Without fail, he would end every single talk with the following statement and question: "I really appreciate what you do for us. Now... what can I do for you?"

An executive of a large corporation was asking a bunch of college students how he could serve them. By just asking this question, he conveyed a more important message—*you are important to me*. Swearingen knew that it was his job as a leader to take care of his people. And as Len Sapera predicted, this gesture made us want to go through walls for him. That is why lasting leaders take care of their people.

Lasting Leaders Listen to Their People

As the operational commander of 150,000 American troops and 20,000 coalition forces, it is without question that Lt. Gen. Vines possessed a great deal of authority in Iraq. In the Pulitzer Prize-winning novel about the Battle of Gettysburg, *The Killer Angels*, Colonel Lawrence Chamberlin remarks, "Generals can do anything. Nothing quite so much like God on earth as a general on a battlefield."[2] After being in Iraq, I can see the truth in this statement. Lt. Gen. Vines made decisions where men died—insurgent and soldier alike.

If any man earned the right to carry this much authority, it was Lt. Gen. Vines. From Panama to Afghanistan to Iraq, I am told that Vines has commanded more troops in combat than any leader in the Department of Defense. Given this experience and his vast authority, it was his decision-making process that always astounded me. He called it Stage One and Stage Two.

During Stage One, Lt. Gen. Vines said that all soldiers should take the rank off their collars and argue about plans and policies. Every soldier, regardless of rank, was honor-bound to share their opinions and disagreements with the boss. He called Stage One the "intellectual knife fight." This is the time where one man must sharpen the other. After the issues were sufficiently debated, Lt. Gen. Vines said we would then enter Stage Two. During Stage Two, we were to put the rank back on our collars, and those in positions to make a decision were to do so smartly.

What he understood is that no one, not even an experienced combat commander like himself, could possibly have every answer. Just because one serves in a position of authority does not mean he is infallible or gifted with perfect foresight or judgment. Given that fact, Lt. Gen. Vines intended to develop a culture within his organization that questioned conventional wisdom and those with high rank.

One of the aims of this culture was to prevent subordinates from simply telling the boss what he wanted to hear. More than anything, it showed that Lt. Gen. Vines was comfortable enough in his own

skin to be wrong. It showed that he was more interested in getting the right answer, than actually being
right. Only through this process could he ensure that
the best decision was made and that the troops in Iraq
were given the best chance to succeed.

Lt. Gen. Vines is right. Lasting leaders listen to
their people.

Lasting Leaders Make Decisive Decisions

All leaders would like to have perfect information. In war, the commander would love to know
exactly where the enemy is and what he is plan-
ning. In business, the CEO would love to know what
new markets the competition plans to enter and with
which products. The reality is that perfect information rarely exists, and the leader who waits for it
will fail. The difficulty in being a leader is making
the best decision given existing uncertainty. That is
why General George S. Patton said, "[A] good plan
violently executed now is better than a perfect plan
next week."[3]

In 2005, General Peter Pace was sworn in as
the Chairman of the Joint Chiefs of Staff. With this
promotion, he became the highest ranking officer in
the Department of Defense and the first Marine ever
to hold this position. In his commencement address
to the 2006 Citadel graduating class, Pace told the
following story about making decisions:

In Vietnam after we spent a couple of
months in Hue City during the Tet of '68, my

company went on a patrol, and my platoon had the lead point on the patrol. I remember getting to the first decision point and calling back on the radio to my company commander and saying, "You want to go left or go right?" And he said, "Go left." I called a second time a little while later and said, "You want me to go left or go right?" He said, "Go right." I called a third time and asked him what he wanted me to do, and I got the butt-chewing of my life over the radio. And basically when you take out the curse words what my company commander said to me was, "Lieutenant, you are in charge—you make the decision."

I handed the radio back to my radio operator, Corporal Irvin, and I said, "If the company commander calls, tell him I'm not here because I'm going to go start making some decisions." And I promised myself that day—38 years ago now—that if I was going to get in trouble again, it was going to be for going too far. And I have gotten in trouble again, and it has been for going too far, and I've had a hard time explaining to my bosses, who were chewing me out, why I was smiling. And I was smiling because I did what I promised myself I would do. I was making decisions.

There is nothing that will demoralize an organization more than a leader that will not exercise the authority of the position and make a decision. The

Marine Corps manual entitled *Warfighting*, states it this way, "We must have the moral courage to make tough decisions in the face of uncertainty—and to accept full responsibility for those decisions—when the natural inclination would be to postpone the decision pending more complete information."[4] Waffling and waiting costs lives in battle and money in business. Leaders have to make decisive decisions and accept the consequences.

General Eisenhower—the Supreme Commander of Allied Forces Europe during World War II—understood this principle well. The day before the allied invasion of Normandy, he penned the following handwritten note for public release, in case the invasion failed.

> Our landings in the Cherbourg-Havre area have failed to gain a satisfactory foothold and I have withdrawn the troops. My decision to attack at this time and place was based upon the best information available. The troops, the air, and the Navy did all that bravery and devotion to duty could do. If any blame or fault attaches to the attempt it is mine alone.[5]

Eisenhower knew that launching an offensive at the beaches of Normandy risked the defeat of the Army and death of his men. The weather was poor—a major issue for an amphibious and airborne assault—and the strength of the enemy unclear. However despite all this uncertainty, he made a decisive decision and accepted the consequences. Subordinates

want to follow leaders who will make the tough decisions. If leaders abdicate this responsibility, subordinates will not follow them for very long. That is why
lasting leaders make decisive decisions.

Lasting Leaders Praise in Public and Counsel in Private

So many leaders violate this rule. They get angry
at subordinates and criticize them in public often via
expletive-laced tirades. While this might help the
boss blow off steam, it erodes his ability to lead. The
recipient of the criticism and those who learn of it
never forget. They take note of the outburst and the
tyrannical conduct. Their confidence in the boss is
shaken because everyone understands that we cannot
master others until we master ourselves.

Instead of this childish behavior, leaders should
take subordinates aside in private before discussing
their failures. These counseling sessions are important
because we all make mistakes. In fact, most learning
is accomplished by taking account of one's mistakes,
and the leader's experience can provide a unique
opportunity to facilitate this learning. However, if
this counseling takes place among the subordinate's
peers, the leader only bites the hand that feeds him
and the organization they both serve.

In public, leaders must only praise the work of
their subordinates. My boss in Iraq was great at this.
I made mistakes all the time. This is only natural,
but sometimes I would make the same mistake twice
which is inexcusable. When I did this, my boss

would take me aside and give me a private butt-chewing. But never did he do this in the presence of my peers or the other leaders of the organization. In front of them, he only highlighted my achievements. For example, if I got something particularly right in an e-mail, he would forward my analysis to our ultimate boss with a tagline, "More great work from Bart Newman..."

This created an environment that fostered learning—one where mistakes were learned from and rarely repeated. As a result, I only made the organization better as I became better at my job. That is why lasting leaders praise in public and counsel in private.

Chapter 5

Fit for the Fight

Do you not know that your body is a temple of the Holy Spirit, who is in you, whom you have received from God? You are not your own.
— 1 Corinthians 6:19

Physical Fitness is not only one of the most important keys to a healthy body, it is the basis of dynamic and creative intellectual activity.
—John F. Kennedy

Our chow hall in Iraq was huge. Think of an all-you-can-eat cafeteria on steroids with a menu to match. There were usually a minimum of two choices of meat (lobster and steak at least once a week), four vegetables, and a choice of bread. There was a large salad bar which had every item that could be found back home and a fully stocked sandwich bar with plenty of snack foods. Furthermore, there was even an entire dessert bar where you could get Baskin-Robbins ice cream, four or five different pies and some of the best cookies I have ever eaten. To drink, we had every option except alcoholic beverages.

We probably ate better than any military in the history of the world. While the menu might have been repetitious, the food was good, and we could have as much as we wanted. Compared to the guys that made the original push into Baghdad two years prior, we were very fortunate.

As the year progressed, I observed an interesting phenomenon in the chow hall—the growing presence of Iraqi officers. As coalition forces gradually built up the Iraqi military, the men who led their forces began to work with us more and more. And it was during mealtime when one could really see how much change was taking place. In the beginning of the deployment, we might have seen a couple of Iraqis eating together from time to time. But near the end, there were so many of them that they took up several tables.

The growing presence of Iraqi officers in the chow hall made us recognize the vast difference in our military cultures. We were mostly from Fort Bragg, the home of the Army's Airborne and Special Forces units, and Fort Bragg is well known for its culture of Physical Training (PT)—a culture that values and puts great emphasis on physical fitness. For example, we began every workday with a formation at 6:25 a.m. Five minutes later, the sound of cannon fire and bugle would echo throughout post signaling reveille. After saluting the flag, we conducted PT until around

7:45 a.m. Our PT consisted of either running at least four miles, doing various exercises to muscle failure, or some combination of both. Before deploying for Iraq, we followed this regimen five days a week.

Without question, Fort Bragg has a PT culture. In fact, one of my bosses summed up the secret to doing well in the Army with one phrase: "Fat is fatal, a bad haircut is bad, and don't be a jerk!" In the chow hall, our "fat is fatal" culture confronted an Iraqi culture with very different values. Many of the senior Iraqi officers were overweight, some even obese. And when they went through the food line, one could see why. They would request additional helpings on plates already piled high with food. And that was not all. After they finished eating and were ready to leave, many would then get a "to go" box. I even saw one overweight Iraqi get a "to go" box crammed with only desserts!

It was very strange for Fort Bragg soldiers to watch any soldier eat like this, even if they were Iraqi. If an American soldier were overweight and acted similarly, he would expect to hear an earful from a superior and maybe even a blunt suggestion to put down the plate. This might seem unkind, but the superior is actually looking out for his soldier. By regulation, the Army is required to expel a soldier if he exceeds certain weight standards.

While we saw lots of Iraqis in the chow hall, the one place I never remember seeing them was in the gym. Every day, our large gym was crammed with service members lifting weights, running on the treadmill, and hitting the punching bag. We would even see the Brits, Koreans, Poles, Australians, Japanese and Italians, but never the Iraqis. It was just a difference in culture.

WHY THE EMPHASIS ON FITNESS?

Seeing this difference in physical fitness prompted me to evaluate why the American military puts so much emphasis on PT. The most obvious reason is because combat is physically demanding. If a buddy gets injured in combat, the soldier needs to have the strength and endurance to carry him off the battle-field. If there is a hand-to-hand fight, the soldier needs to have the quickness and power to defeat his adversary. That being said, most soldiers will never carry a comrade off the field or come within striking distance of the enemy. My leaders knew this, and yet even in the middle of a combat zone, they constantly stressed the importance of PT and continued to eval-uate our fitness.

Ultimately, the American military stresses phys-ical fitness because it produces much more than a healthy body. Through exertion and sweat, it molds the entire person. The Army Field Manual puts it this way, "Physically fit people feel more competent and confident, handle stress better, work longer and harder, and recover faster."[1] While thinking about this issue in Iraq, I made a similar conclusion which I recorded in my journal—exercise is important because it develops a keen mind, a strong will, and self-confidence in all endeavors.

My own life had already convinced me of this point. I had always been an athlete and physically active. After playing several sports throughout childhood, I focused on tennis because I thought it afforded me the greatest chance to play in college. By the time I graduated from high school, I was one of the better players in my state and received a few scholarship offers to play at the next level. I turned them down and instead "walked-on" at the University of Georgia, one of the best teams in the country. During tryouts, it became clear I probably was not good enough to be on the team. But because my coach was a generous man and I worked hard, he let me stay. Essentially, I became the "Rudy" of Georgia Tennis—the guy that practiced hard but rode the bench during the game. In fact, I only played in two regular season matches— winning one and losing the other.

While I might not have cracked the starting lineup, my team excelled. Our guys were some of the greatest players in the world. We won two Southeastern Conference (SEC) Championships, and one year made it to the National Collegiate Athletic Association (NCAA) finals, only to fall short and finish second in the nation. However, this success in the spring was the result of some incredibly hard practices starting with "two-a-days" in August. I remember a teammate vomiting once on the court, and I left almost every practice so exhausted I felt like doing the same. But through constant exhaustion, I reached the height of my physical fitness.

Interestingly, it was during this time I also had the most success off the tennis court. Despite practicing at least twenty hours a week, I was elected president of the Student Government. The next year, which was my busiest with the team, I achieved a perfect 4.0 grade point average—the only year in my life I enjoyed such an academic accomplishment. I would have thought that being busy with tennis would have diminished my ability to excel in other areas, but it enhanced it. Because I was fit, I actually thought better, could work harder, and achieved greater success in all my endeavors.

However, after tearing ligaments in my knee during a flag-football game, this would change. I underwent ACL reconstructive surgery, and although my knee was supposed to be as good as new, I had no confidence in my physical abilities. What I did not realize was that this loss of physical confidence led to a loss of confidence in other areas. Because I was afraid to push myself on the athletic field, I found that I lost mental acuity and a will to push myself off the athletic field.

It was not until joining the Army that I fully understood this. The Army did not give me a choice. During PT, the Army required me to physically exert myself again. It required me to run hard and push my body further than I thought I could. Once I arrived at Fort Bragg, the Army sent me to Airborne School where they pushed me even harder. Only at Airborne School, they worked us to physical exhaustion, and then shoved us out of airplanes! I can think of few things worse for a bad knee than hitting the ground at twenty-two feet per second (or fifteen miles per hour), the speed at which you land under the canopy of a T-10D parachute. But the knee held, and my confidence in it and myself grew.

This confidence continued to grow in Iraq. Despite working incredibly long hours, I made time to work out. As I got stronger in the gym, I felt stronger to tackle all the craziness of that year. It is a principle: exercise increases our capacity to achieve. As we push ourselves to achieve more than we think is possible in the gym, we actually grow the confidence to achieve more than we think is possible in all other areas of life.

DOES GOD CARE ABOUT OUR FITNESS AND FOOD?

When I sat down to write this book, I asked myself whether God really cares if we eat right and are physically fit. I know God wants our hearts to reflect His. I know that He wants an intimate relationship with us. But does He really care about our fitness and food?

For the Christian, I believe He does. Speaking to the church in Corinth, the apostle Paul asked, "Do you not know that your body is a temple of the Holy Spirit, who is in you, whom you have received from God? You are not your own" (1 Cor. 6:19). According to Scripture, our bodies are not really our own, but are the temple in which He dwells. Therefore, when we fail to exercise and eat well, I believe we damage the temple. Over time, we hammer away at the temple's foundation until the building crumbles to the ground, and we die. If we do not take care of our bodies, we limit our usefulness to God because we either die early or become too weak to serve.

Rupert Pelham Wesson, Jr. was my maternal grandfather and one of the kindest men I have ever known. He was fiercely loyal to his family and the community in which he was born and raised. I loved him and called him Granddaddy. When he went into the hospital for triple bypass surgery, my brother and I went to visit him. Years of smoking, overeating and little exercise had taken its toll on his arteries. Thankfully, he had a peace about the operation. He told me that although he was not ready to die, he trusted the Lord and was prepared to go if that was His will. After surgery, we went to see him again. He was in a great mood and explained all the changes he planned to make to his lifestyle. By doctor's orders, he was going to start exercising and eating a lot healthier. As I encouraged him to do so, he gave me a wicked smile and said, "But boy, God wouldn't have made fried chicken so good if he didn't want us to eat it!"

Sadly, my grandfather died just a few days later from post-surgery complications. This was an enormous loss for my family because he was such a wonderful man, and we needed him. To this day, it pains me that he never knew my children. But more important, it was a loss for the Lord. He lost a laborer in the field. Because of unhealthy habits, God prematurely lost someone that made a difference in this world for Him.

THE BATTLE WITH THE ALARM CLOCK

God wants us to exercise and eat right because it extends our lives and makes us fit for the fight. By exercising and eating properly, our bodies are able to go wherever and do whatever God needs. The only question is whether we will do it, whether we will muster the will to make it happen.

I refer to this test of the will as the battle with the alarm clock. Since getting out of the Army, my job no longer requires me to be at a 6:25 a.m. formation. Instead of getting up early to exercise, I can just press snooze and return to blissful sleep. But when I do, I suffer my defeat for the rest of the day. The alarm clock beat me. I was not strong enough to deny the temptation of the snooze and get my tail up.

After knee surgery, but before joining the Army, I suffered defeat constantly. I would make plans to start a workout routine, but after a couple of good mornings, would succumb to the temptation of the snooze. I would then try accountability and convince my buddies to meet me early in the morning. Well, they would show up, but I would not. Of course, I deserved and received a great deal of razzing for this weakness. And with a smile, I had to suffer my defeat again and again.

The Army showed me that victory over the alarm clock is worth the price. Whatever pain is induced by answering the alarm's call, in no way compares to the feeling of victory I enjoy the rest of the day. When I defeat the alarm clock, I walk with my head up. It gives me an edge on the day and produces a quiet confidence that strengthens my will to tackle life's other challenges.

IF SKINNY CAN, SO CAN WE

Theodore Roosevelt is remembered today as a former president, conservationist, explorer, hunter, and soldier. It was during the Spanish American War where Roosevelt and his Rough Riders famously attacked a fortified hill to outflank and defeat the Spanish in San Juan, Cuba. This act of heroism was so remarkable that the men on the ground claimed that he deserved the Congressional Medal of Honor.[2] Following two terms in the White House, Roosevelt sailed to Africa to go on a safari. After killing 296 big-game animals, including nine lions, he would return home only to be shot in the chest while running for president again. In their book, *The Roosevelts: An American Saga*, Peter Collier and David Horowitz recount the incident:

At a campaign stop in Milwaukee on the evening of October 14, 1912, a deranged former bartender…emerged from a crowd and shot TR point-blank in the chest. Buckling from the impact, TR righted himself and calmly put his hand inside his coat to verify that he was bleeding. "They have pinked me," he said, and then put his hand to his mouth and coughed. Seeing no arterial blood, he calculated that he was not hit in the lungs and the wound was probably therefore not fatal…He told aids who were clamoring for him to go to a hospital, "You get me to that speech. It may be the last one I shall deliver and I am going to deliver this one myself." Bleeding heavily, he began his appearance by gesturing at the crowd. "Friends, I should ask you to be as quiet as possible. I don't know if you fully understand that I have just been shot, but it takes more than that to kill a Bull Moose."[3]

Although he would lose this race for a third term, this Bull Moose would recover from the shooting and embark on other adventures, including exploring uncharted lands in Brazil. Just prior to his death in 1919, his son Archie had returned home from World War I after being injured. Of Roosevelt's other three sons, two were still serving in Germany and the other, a pilot, had been shot down and killed behind enemy lines. After Roosevelt died, Archie sent word to his two brothers in Germany with the following one-sentence telegram: "The old lion is dead."[4]

Roosevelt died affectionately known as the "old lion." What few know is that he did not start life that way. As a small boy, his family called him "Skinny" because of his small frame and weak health. He had terrible asthma attacks that closed off his lungs and threatened his life. During such episodes, the family would take him on wild carriage rides to try to force air into his failing lungs. He suffered from dysentery and was severely nearsighted. Despite taking him to doctors all over the world, nothing seemed to help.

At age fourteen, after being physically bullied by other boys, Roosevelt's father told him, "Theodore, you have the mind but you have not the body, and without the help of the body the mind cannot go as far as it should."[5] At his father's urging, Roosevelt began boxing, lifting weights, and riding horses. He used exercise to push his body, which gradually transformed his "Skinny" frame into that of a robust man. Because of that transformation, Roosevelt came to believe in what he called the "strenuous life"—that only by continuously pushing the body can a person become all that he should.

Few of us started life with as many weaknesses as Theodore Roosevelt, and even fewer have taken a bullet and then made a speech. For those that have struggled with physical difficulties, his life should serve as an inspiration. For the rest of us, it should serve as a kick in the tail. We will not become all that God wants unless we take care of our bodies, the temple that holds His spirit. We must win the victory over the alarm clock and live the "strenuous life" so that we may become fit for the fight. In so doing, we can serve God more fully.

Chapter 6

Financially Free

The rich rule over the poor, and the borrower is servant to the lender.

— Prov. 22:7

Make all you can, save all you can, give all you can.

—John Wesley

To my surprise, there were several opportunities for soldiers to spend money in Iraq. On our sprawling base, there were two Post Exchanges (PXs). One of these was even the size of a small Wal-Mart and contained many of the same goods. There were clothes, snack foods, and a variety of electronic devices for sale, including big screen TVs, cameras, DVD players, laptop computers, and video game consoles. In addition to the two PXs, there were bazaars that sold jewelry, artwork, and other crafts from the Middle East. Fast food restaurants operating out of single-wide trailers abounded. There was a SUBWAY, Burger King, Pizza Hut, Cinnabon, and a fried chicken restaurant. And if that was not enough, one could buy a $4 cappuccino from the gourmet coffee shop.

I mostly found this troubling. Every day there was a line of young soldiers waiting outside these establishments, particularly the coffee shop and restaurants. It just seemed like such a waste of money especially since they could have gotten basically the same coffee, sandwich, and pizza in the chow hall, for free!

Most of these soldiers did not make a lot of money. However, because the military paid for every necessity in the combat zone (food, clothing, and shelter) the deployment actually presented a great financial opportunity for them. In fact, single soldiers could have saved almost every penny they earned for an entire year. Unfortunately, many of them needed to.

Before deploying for Iraq, I spent several months on Fort Bragg providing legal assistance. Any soldier that wanted to talk with a lawyer could make an appointment with me or one of my colleagues free of charge. Unfortunately, a large portion of our clients came to discuss their financial problems. Their stories had a common theme: they had used credit to buy items they could no longer afford. For example, one soldier bought a house using creative financing, but after a bit of bad luck, could neither make the payments, nor sell the property. Another financed an expensive car that looked good, but ran poorly. Others naively abused credit cards believing that as long as they made minimum payments, every-thing would work out. Now creditors were calling, not only at home, but also at work. The soldiers, and their spouses, suffered. Across from my desk, I could see visible heartache in their faces. They hoped I could somehow fix the mess, but all I could offer was a way out that would require time, discipline, and sacrifice.

Soldiers are not the only ones spending more than they make. Unfortunately, it is a problem that perme-ates every community in the country regardless of race, region, or religion. The Commerce Department recently confirmed this fact reporting that the 2006 U.S. savings rate was negative 1 percent, the lowest level since the Great Depression.[1] This means that in 2006, Americans spent 1 percent more than they made. There have only been three other years in American history with a negative savings rate: 2005, 1933, and 1932. The last two years correspond to the middle of the Great Depression. At that time, Americans were understandably spending more than they made just to provide food, clothing, and shelter—basic needs. Today, the negative savings rate is a product of some-thing quite different. We are spending more than we make to buy gourmet dinners, designer clothing, and luxurious homes—extravagant wants.

Our government has not been doing any better. In fiscal year 2006, Congress spent $248 billion more than it had in the treasury.[2] Because this has been going on for years, the country is now $8.7 tril-lion dollars in debt. A sum so great that every man, woman, and child would have to write a check for $29,000 just to get us back to even.

We are hemorrhaging red ink, and it is unjustified. We cannot blame our debt on low income because we are the wealthiest people in the history of the world. Even the average poor American has a higher living standard than the average world citizen (this is the average world citizen, not even poor world citizen).[3] The problem is not our income, it is our spending. We have the wrong attitude about money in that we have confused the difference between what we want and what we need. There is nothing wrong with satisfying our wants from time to time, but when we fail to recognize the difference, we make purchases that we cannot afford which leads to debt with which we cannot live.

THE GENIUS OF MARKETING

This confusion is largely the product of great marketing campaigns. In a sense, we are simply victims of our own genius. Whenever we turn on the TV, go to the mall, or open the mailbox we are bombarded by commercials, displays, and catalogs that present many alluring items. Before long, these items are not only nice, they seem like necessities. In his book *Your Money Counts*, Howard Dayton illustrates how effective great marketing can be:

An American company opened a new plant in Central America because labor was plentiful and inexpensive. The opening of the plant proceeded smoothly until the workers at the plant received their first paychecks. The next day none of the villagers reported to work. The plant manager went to see the village chief to talk about the problem. "Why should we continue to work?" the chief asked in response to the manager's inquiry. "We are satisfied. We have already earned all the money we need to live on."

The plant stood idle for two months until someone came up with the bright idea of sending a mail-order catalog to every villager. Reading the catalogs created new desires for the villagers. Soon they returned to work, and there has been no employment problem since then.[4]

I am as susceptible to this as anyone else. Once a marketing campaign transforms a product in my mind from nice to necessary, it is just a matter of time before I craft a rationale to justify the purchase. For example, after returning from Iraq, I was sitting on my couch one evening flipping through channels on the television. I came across the home shopping network and paused. There was Esteban, the world famous guitar player, wearing his signature black outfit and black hat—he basically resembles the movie character Zorro, but wears black sunglasses instead of the black mask. He was playing some great music with his band and for only a few hundred dollars, was willing to sell one of his guitars.

I have always loved music and wanted to play the guitar. As I listened to Esteban describe the crafts-manship of this instrument and play it so well, I was sold. I then crafted a justification in my mind telling myself that I would use the guitar to introduce music to my children—I mean, music promotes early brain development, right?

When Julie walked into the room, I had the phone in one hand and my credit card in the other. I told her what I wanted to do. She smiled and then asked, "Do you need it?" I kind of stuttered a second and then offered my justification of how it would be good for the kids. She then asked, "Do you think you'll have enough time to play?" This one hit harder. Our newborn's nocturnal schedule had left little time for sleep, much less anything else. As I continued to roll her question around in my mind, I knew she was right. I certainly did not need the guitar and probably would not use it. Her wise words saved me.

WHAT DOES GOD SAY ABOUT MONEY AND POSSESSIONS?

During my last year of law school, Julie and I participated in a Bible study produced by Crown Financial Ministries. The purpose of the study was to examine what God had to say about money and possessions. Although I was knowledgeable about personal finance, I was unaware that the Bible said anything on the subject. I read all the financial maga-zines (*Kiplinger's*; *Money*; etc.) and books (*Rich Dad, Poor Dad*; *Think and Grow Rich*; etc.), but I never thought to read the Bible for advice on personal finance.

As it turned out, the study showed me that God had a lot to say about our money and possessions. In fact, Jesus said more about money than almost any other subject. The Bible contains more than 2,350 verses on money and possessions, while fewer than 500 verses on such subjects as faith and prayer.[5] As I began to study these verses, I learned why. Jesus had to talk about money because the way we spend it reflects the priorities of our heart. Jesus said, "For where your treasure is, there your heart will be also" (Matt. 6:21). Andy Stanley put it this way, "If you want to know what is really important to someone, just open their checkbook and see where they spend their money."

Over the course of the study, I slowly developed a different perspective on money, a biblical perspective; this new perspective illuminated for me three principles of Scripture.

1) Our money and possessions are not really ours, they belong to God. The Bible says, "Yours, O Lord, is the greatness and the power and the glory and the majesty and the splendor, for everything in heaven and earth is yours" (1 Chron. 29:11-12). God owns it all. We are just stewards of His wealth and possessions. Because we are nothing more than God's money managers, we should evaluate our spending decisions through this perspective. We should ask whether our spending glorifies God and whether our possessions further His work. As our spending prior-

ities come to reflect God's priorities, our hearts will begin to reflect His.

2) We should give a percentage of our income directly to God. The Old Testament says that "[a] tithe of everything from the land, whether grain from the soil or fruit from the trees, belongs to the Lord; it is holy to the Lord" (Lev. 27:30). A tithe is simply a tenth. Unlike the Old Testament, the New Testament does not specify a certain percentage, but repeatedly highlights the necessity to support God's work on earth. Jesus said, "Give to Caesar what is Caesar's, and to God what is God's" (Matt. 22:21). I believe that we should give at least 10 percent of our gross earnings to the church. However, the percentage is far less important to the Lord than the attitude in which it is given. Because regardless of what amount God directs us to give, this act of obedience helps us to sever our ties to this world. It reminds us that we have a home, and it is not the one where we pick up our mail.

3) Being in debt is akin to being a slave. The Bible says, "The rich rule over the poor, and the borrower is servant to the lender" (Prov. 22:7). While Scripture does not say that being in debt is a sin, it strongly cautions against it. Of these three principles, this one was the most difficult for me. Because I subscribed to the world's view of personal finance, I viewed debt as a tool. I thought there was good debt (i.e., debt that authorizes a tax deduction like home mortgages) and then bad debt (i.e., credit

card balances, car payments, etc.). I figured that as long as I stayed away from the bad and embraced the good, I would get ahead financially. While the math confirms this logic, God has a different perspective. God says that when we are in debt, we are slaves to our lenders.

To be clear, I believe a home mortgage can be permissible debt if the property could be sold quickly for more than the mortgage payment—this is typically the case when we make the purchase in conjunction with a 20 percent down payment. But I also believe that God wants us to work aggressively to pay off all personal debt, including our home mortgages. While we might lose a tax deduction, we gain our freedom from the slavery of debt which allows us to serve wherever and whenever God calls us.

PUTTING THESE PRINCIPLES INTO PRACTICE

After taking the Crown Bible study, I started to read books by authors with a biblical perspective on personal finance. In Iraq of all places, I ordered books by Dave Ramsey, Ron Blue, Austin Pryor, Howard Dayton, and Larry Burkett. These men dedicate hundreds of pages to the subject of how to put biblical principles on personal finance into practice. They each have a system for getting out of debt, saving for the future, and living the life God calls us to live.

Once I returned home, I used their advice to create a system for my family. However, when I tried to put it in practice, I learned that certain habits were not working for Julie and me. After a few discussions, we made adjustments to the system and found something that works for us. Our three-step system is below.

Take an Audit

Every public corporation audits its books. These businesses know exactly how much money comes in the door and how much goes out. They know what they spend their money on so they can evaluate whether the expense is justified.

Everyone thinks it is wise for a business to audit their books, yet few ever apply this discipline to their own personal finances. I was one of them. To my detriment, I rarely balanced my checkbook, much less examined where I spent every penny for a given month. However, as I developed a biblical perspective on personal finance, I realized that it was necessary.

As a result, Julie and I began saving every receipt and bank statement we received. After a couple of months, I pulled out these pieces of paper and added up what we spent on everything from gasoline, to eating out, to income and payroll taxes. I then grabbed a sample budget spreadsheet off the Internet and entered the data.

We were shocked. When my wife and I examined the totals, we could not believe how much we were spending on things like entertainment and going out to eat. We were even surprised to learn that we had spent a few more dollars than we made in certain months. This exercise made us examine the facts. The numbers showed exactly how we were living and spending. With these facts, we could then take action.

Decide Where the Money Will Go

When I was a kid, I used to keep my money in a Mason jar. As odd as it sounds, I still think Mason jars provide a useful tool for picturing how we should distribute our income. In Jar 1, we place 10 percent of our gross income and use it for tithing. This money belongs to God, and we pay Him first. Jar 2 is ultimately for saving, and we use 15 to 20 percent of our gross income to fill it. (We will discuss Jar 2 shortly.) In Jar 3, we put the rest of our income and use it to pay all our life expenses. This includes such expenses as taxes, groceries, and all our debts.

Time to return to Jar 2. Many of us decide to follow God's rules for money after making several decisions outside of that guidance. As a result, we often have no personal savings and are drowning in debt. That is where Jar 2 comes in. This jar should first be used to save three months of living expenses. This money is an emergency fund and belongs in an interest-bearing checking account or money market fund that does not incur penalties for withdrawal. Without this emergency fund, we are in a place where life's setbacks can cause financial ruin. For example, if we lose our job, we should be able to support ourselves without going into debt. An emergency fund makes this possible.

Once we have three months of living expenses saved, we need to use Jar 2 to pay off our consumer debts—that is, all debts besides our home mortgage on which we have made a 20 percent down payment. We should make a list of all our debts, with the least amount at the top and the most at the bottom. We should then dedicate Jar 2 to the smallest debt, the one on the top of the list. Once these extra payments eliminate that debt, we then dedicate Jar 2 to the next debt on the list and continue until all of our personal debts are paid.

Many resist this rule of thumb, especially if a small debt has a low interest rate and a big debt has a higher one. Their objection is that they would save more money by dedicating Jar 2 to eliminating the highest interest rate debts first. While that might be true, tackling the smallest debts first provides a victory. These victories, even if small at first, encourage us to believe that with God's help, we can actually become debt-free. As such, I recommend adhering to this rule of thumb.

However, once we have eliminated all debt besides the home mortgage, we can start using Jar 2 for its real purpose, saving for the future. This money should be invested in a vehicle like the stock market that has a long track record of significant appreciation. In fact, the broad stock market has averaged an annual return of 10 percent since its inception. While the stock market certainly goes down, there is still no ten-year period in its history where it did not produce a positive return. That being said, if money is likely to be needed within ten years, a less volatile investment like bonds might be preferable. We have to remember the point of this money. It is our nest egg in old age — money that will allow us to pay for expenses in case we can no longer work or choose not to.

Once we start using Jar 2 to take care of the future, we can employ Jar 3 on our home mortgage. By this point, this debt should be the only one we owe. Instead of now using Jar 3 to improve our life-style and enjoy the good life, we should use it to make extra payments on the mortgage. If we dedicate ourselves to this goal, we will soon replace the bank as the real owner of our home.

Pay Cash

If we use credit cards and do not pay them off every month, plastic surgery is necessary — grab a sturdy pair of scissors and just start cutting! By living only on cash, we prevent ourselves from spending more than we have. Besides halting overspending, plastic surgery has an additional benefit — it saves money. People who use cash actually spend less than those who use plastic even if they pay off their bills every month.

I used to be a credit card guy. I would use my cash-back card to earn at least 1 percent on my purchases and then pay the bill off every month. By my calculation, I earned a couple of hundred dollars a year from my credit card company. However, while sitting on my bunk in Iraq, I came across an interesting story in Ron Blue's book, *Master Your Money,* which changed my thinking on this subject. In the book, Blue tells about reading one day that credit cards cause a family to spend 34 percent more a year even if they pay off the balance every month. Because he thought this was absurd, Blue decided to spend a year trying to disprove it. The following is what happened:

So Judy and I put away our credit cards and lived strictly on cash. We paid cash for everything.

By using cash throughout the year, my spending mentality changed. It was much more difficult to pay $25 for a tank of gas using cash than if I used a credit card. (I still had the Olds 98, affectionately labeled "Old Blue.") Paying cash at the drugstore caused me, at the very least, to hesitate, and in most cases, to eliminate those impulsive purchases at the checkout counter. Paying cash for clothes caused me to think very seriously about the need for such items. Paying cash for car repairs caused me to examine whether it could be done less expensively, either by myself or at another place. Paying cash for airplane tickets while traveling caused me to think a second time about the trip I was taking.

The conclusion of the story is that after living on a straight cash budget for a year, without using credit cards at all, our living expenses decreased by 33 percent from a level I had thought was "bare bones" to begin with.[6]

When I got home from Iraq, my wife and I began to implement this all-cash system, and I am convinced that it saves us money. We simply go to the bank and withdraw all the money that our monthly budget allocates to discretionary spending (i.e., groceries, eating out, entertainment, gifts to friends, vet bills, etc.). When the money runs out—and sometimes it does—we simply hold out until the beginning of the following month. Actually, we have found that running out of money teaches us discipline. The discomfort of going without something encourages us to spend more wisely in the future.

We follow another habit that some find interesting. I give all this discretionary cash to my wife. When we first began the all-cash plan, I would question Julie constantly about her purchases. Did our daughter really need a new shirt? Did we really need to take the minivan to the carwash? Do we really need organic milk? My questioning, however, was giving my wife unneeded anxiety. It became clear I had taken my zeal to get out of debt too far. Now, Julie manages all discretionary income while I use online banking to pay the mortgage, car insurance, and other fixed monthly payments. When I want to eat out with my friends, I have to get the money from her. When I want a new pair of running shoes, I talk with my wife. The beauty of this system is that Julie is now an equal participant in our plan instead of just being held captive by it. We now plan our purchases together which makes for wiser decisions.

SLAY THE BEAST!

For most of us, this plan is challenging. Giving God at least 10 percent and saving another 15-20 percent will require discipline and sacrifice. For those of us who are borderline bankrupt, however, it will take even more. Those folks could not set aside 25-30 percent of their gross income for giving and investing no matter how much discipline they employed. For those, more drastic measures are needed.

First, they need to realize that they have an enemy. This enemy is every bit as threatening and nasty as a wild beast. No matter how often it is fed, the beast is never satisfied. It always wants something newer, shinier, or more expensive. Simply put, this beast is our consumptive lifestyle. And because it threatens to devour us, we must slay it.

Nowhere can one better see the beast run wild than in a TV commercial by LendingTree, the online lending and realty services exchange. The commercial opens with an average-looking man named Stanley Johnson standing with his wife and kids. Stanley then starts to describe all the amenities of his suburban life. He shows off his brand new SUV, points out his beautiful four bedroom home, and even boasts about his membership in the local golf club. In every way, Stanley appears to be living the American dream. But finally, Stanley reveals the secret to all his success. He looks into the camera and asks, "How do I do it? I'm in debt up to my eyeballs! I can barely pay my finance charges!" And then with a smile still plastered to his face, he pleads into the camera, "Somebody help me!"

Many of us live this painful reality. Just like Stanley Johnson, we are so helplessly in debt that we live a life of silent desperation. Through credit, we have bought new cars, beautiful houses, and memberships to the golf club. But because we can barely afford the payments, these items are no longer a source of enjoyment, only pain. However, because we are embarrassed, we do not tell anyone and simply force a smile as if nothing is wrong. We are paralyzed and fail to take desperate action because it will publicize our failure to our friends and colleagues. If we sell the new SUV and buy an old, inexpensive sedan, we would be forced to explain what happened. So we buy lottery tickets and pray for a miracle.

This silent desperation must end. That is not God's intent for our lives. We must seek help and ask for God's strength to take some drastic measures. God does not care if we are embarrassed; He just wants us to be free. But to be free, we must get aggressive. In most cases, that means we must sell expensive items and use the proceeds to pay off debt. Some of us need to sell our home and downsize to something more affordable. Some need to sell a boat, snowmobile, or other recreational vehicle. But for most of us, we just need to sell the car.

Those that are in serious debt usually get there by buying a car they cannot afford. Nowhere is this truer than on Fort Bragg. Because the Army provides a steady paycheck, car dealerships are always willing to lend money to soldiers. As a result, I often met soldiers who made $30,000 a year, and yet bought SUVs with a $40,000 sticker price. One of my colleagues once had such a soldier in his office that made such a purchase. The soldier was now drowning in debt and was looking for help. My colleague told him that in order to avoid bankruptcy, he needed to sell the SUV. Facing this tragedy, the soldier just said, "I can't do that…I have to have my SUV!"

Dr. Thomas Stanley and Dr. William Danko wrote one of the most enlightening books I have ever read: *The Millionaire Next Door*. This international best seller investigates the spending habits of those Americans who have a net worth exceeding one million dollars. In the book, they dedicate an entire chapter to the automobiles millionaires drive, entitled "You Aren't What You Drive."

Their study found that the typical millionaire paid $24,800 for his most recent automobile purchase. Of those millionaires, 37 percent bought a used vehicle. At the same time, the average American who purchased a new vehicle paid $21,000 for their most recent acquisition.[7] Somehow 37 percent of millionaires feel that a used vehicle is adequate for their use, yet many near bankrupt Americans insist on buying only new. Stanley and Danko are right. We are not what we drive. If the average millionaire does not drive an expensive new car, then those with less money should feel comfortable doing the same.

Sell the expensive car. Buy something inexpensive and use the proceeds to pay off debt. This will help rein in the consumptive lifestyle and slay the beast. Once we are no longer living to pay off debt, we can start using our finances to live for God.

Chapter 7

Making Marriage Matter

For this reason a man will leave his father
and mother and be united to his wife, and
they will become one flesh.
                                    —Genesis 2:24

A day not married is a day wasted!
                                    —Dan Cathy

Sullivan Ballou was born on March 28, 1829, to a
distinguished Huguenot family from Smithfield,
Rhode Island. He was educated at some of America's
most prestigious institutions (Phillips Academy in
Andover, Massachusetts, and Brown University
in Providence, Rhode Island). He was a lawyer by
trade, but was more prominently known as a young
statesman. He was only twenty-eight when members
of the Rhode Island House of Representatives
unanimously elected him as their Speaker—the
highest position of leadership in the House.

Despite political prominence and professional promise, the outbreak of the Civil War in April of 1861 prompted Ballou to choose another path. The government was raising regiments for Federal service, and although his position did not require participation, he felt it his duty to serve. The decision to volunteer, however, would require great personal sacrifice. He would have to leave the home he built, the wife he loved, and the two small boys—Edgar (age 4) and William (age 2)—he cherished. As he contemplated imminent battle, Ballou wrote a letter to his wife, excerpts of which are found below:[1]

July 14, 1861.
Camp Clark, Washington

My Very Dear Sarah,

The indications are very strong that we shall move in a few days — perhaps tomorrow. Lest I should not be able to write again, I feel impelled to write a few lines that may fall under your eye when I shall be no more. Our movements may be of a few days duration and full of pleasure — and it may be one of severe conflict and death to me. Not my will, but thine, O God be done...

Sarah my love for you is deathless, it seems to bind me with mighty cables, that nothing but Omnipotence could break; and yet my love of Country comes over me like a strong wind, and bears me irresistibly on with all those chains, to the battle field. The memories of all the blissful moments I have spent with you, come creeping over me, and I feel most gratified to God and you that I have enjoyed them so long. And how hard it is for me to give them up and burn to ashes the hopes of future years, when, God willing we might still have lived and loved together, and seen our boys grow up to honorable manhood around us. I have, I know, but few and small claims upon Divine Providence, but something whispers to me — perhaps it is the wafted prayer of my little Edgar, that I shall return to my loved ones unharmed. If I do not, my dear Sarah, never forget how much I love you, and when my last breath escapes me on the battle field, it will whisper your name...

But, O Sarah! if the dead can come back to this earth and flit unseen around those they loved, I shall always be near you; in the gladest days and the darkest nights, advised to your happiest scenes and gloomiest hours, always, always; and if there be a soft breeze upon your cheek, it shall be my breath, or the cool air cools your throbbing temple, it shall be my spirit passing by. Sarah do not mourn me dead; think I am gone and wait for thee, for we shall meet again.

As for my little boys — they will grow up as I have done, and never know a father's love and care. Little Willie is too young to remember me long — and my blue eyed Edgar will keep my frolics with him among the dimmest memories of his childhood. Sarah, I have unlimited confidence in your maternal care and your development of their characters, and feel that God will bless you in your holy work.

Tell my two Mothers I call God's blessings upon them new. O! Sarah I wait for you there; come to me, and lead thither my children.

Sullivan

Just a few days after writing this letter, Sullivan Ballou was killed at the First Battle of Bull Run.

If there is a more beautiful and endearing testament of a husband's love for his wife, I am unaware of it. To inspire such an honest, timeless statement, Sullivan and Sarah must have had a powerful marriage. Thankfully, the God of the universe wants the same for us.[2] The author and inventor of marriage wants us to experience this kind of love, passion, and devotion. We know this because the Bible compares the relationship of a husband and a wife to that of Christ and his bride, the church. The Bible says, "Husbands, love your wives, just as Christ loved the church and gave himself up for her to make her holy, cleansing her by the washing with water through the word, and to present her to himself as a radiant church, without blemish, but holy and blameless" (Eph. 5:25-26).

The love Christ showed for the church was not an ordinary love. It was not weak or wanting. It was a love so bold and passionate that He endured torture and then death on a cross. Yet, this extreme love is what husbands are supposed to have for their wives. God wants there to be no greater love on earth than that which exists in the marriage relationship.

But God wants us to have even more than that. Besides unparalleled love, He wants total interdependence. Jesus says, "For this reason a man will leave his father and mother and be united to his wife, and the two will become one flesh. So they are no longer two, but one" (Mark 10:7-8).

It was not until I deployed to Iraq that I could fully understand this description of marriage. Before then, I always viewed the reference to "one flesh" as mostly an allusion to sexual union. But during my year in Iraq, I realized it is much more. At the time I deployed, Julie and I had been married a little more than four years, but I did not understand how interdependent we had become. The interdependence was such that when in Iraq, I always felt like something was not right. From the time I woke up in the morning until I went to bed at night, there was a feeling of loss.

General Thomas J. Jackson is one of the most celebrated commanders in American military history. It was at the Battle of Bull Run—the first major battle of the Civil War and the one that claimed Sullivan Ballou's life—that General Jackson's legend was born. The advancing Union Army had the Confederates in retreat until General Jackson's troops arrived on the field and checked their advance. Watching General Jackson repel the Union attack, General Bernard E. Bee proclaimed, "There is Jackson standing like a stone wall!" The Confederate Army would go on to route the Union forces earning General Jackson the nickname "Stonewall."

Less than two years later, General Stonewall Jackson was wounded at the Battle of Chancellorsville, which required the immediate amputation of his left arm. However, while recovering from his wounds, he caught pneumonia and died days later. In the intervening time between his injury and death, Jackson's commander, General Robert E. Lee, would say, "He has lost his left arm; but I have lost my right."

For some reason, I came across this statement while I was in Iraq. As I began to ponder Lee's words and how well the metaphor illustrated his dependence on Jackson, I found direct relevance to my marriage. Being away from my wife was like asking me to do without my right arm. Because we were one flesh—because we were so interdependent—I never felt whole. Something was always missing. On January 18, 2006, I made the following entry in my journal: "[Julie] has become such a part of me that I just don't feel like myself without her. It's like someone removed a piece of my soul and asked me to do without it for a year. I could and I did, but I never felt right and always felt the loss."

HOW IS MARRIAGE DOING?

God wants us to experience a marriage of love, passion, and devotion. I also believe that He wants us to have a marriage of such interdependence that we feel like we are separated from our own flesh, when separated from our spouse. If God wants this for us—and we want it for ourselves—one would think that the institution of marriage would be thriving. Unfortunately, the reality is far different.

According to new statistics compiled by the Census Bureau, for the first time in U.S. history married couples no longer make up the majority of households. In fact, only 49.7 percent of the nation's households in 2005 were made up of married couples.[3] The decline in marriage has been steady. In 2000, 52 percent of U.S. households were married couples, while in 1990, it was 56 percent, and in 1930, it was 84 percent.[4] Over the last seventy-five years, there has been almost a 35 percent decline in the number of married households.

Three factors have led to the decline of marriage. First, about 45 percent of U.S. marriages end in divorce—the highest such rate in the world.[5] Second, more couples are now choosing to cohabitate—meaning they are unmarried, yet share a sexual relationship and live in the same household.[6] Interestingly, these cohabitating couples break up at a much higher rate than even married couples.[7] Finally, more Americans are choosing to stay single than at any previous time.[8] Because there is no end in sight to these trends, the institution of marriage is likely to continue its decline in the coming decades.

CONSEQUENCES

The decline of marriage is a tragedy, especially for children. Because of the already high divorce rate, even higher breakup rate among cohabitating couples, and recent increase in out-of-wedlock births, more children are being raised today in single parent homes than at any time in history. In fact the Census Bureau's 2005 statistics show that 28 percent of children lived in single parent homes in 2005, while only 9 percent did in 1960. This is more than a threefold increase in the span of forty-five years. In their book, *Growing Up With a Single Parent*, Professors Sarah McLanahan and Gary Sandefur use four national surveys and more than a decade of research to examine the life outcomes of single parent children. Compared to those children who live with both parents, they found that single parent children were about twice as likely to be poor, to not graduate from high school, and to have an unwed birth.[9] This research forced them to make the following conclusion:

Children who grow up in a household with only one biological parent are worse off, on average, than children who grow up in a household with both of their biological parents, regardless of the parents' race or educational background, regardless of

120

whether the parents are married when the child is born, and regardless of whether the resident parent remarries.[10]

This research describes something that we intuitively know to be true. Because of the breakdown of the family, children suffer. This only makes sense because raising children is such a difficult job. But marriage, more than any other social organization, ensures that the two people who have the greatest vested interest in seeing their children succeed are present to partake in that time-consuming task. Without that social arrangement, one parent usually assumes the job of two.

Because my parents divorced, I am particularly passionate about this subject. It was the summer after second grade, and because they argued and at times talked about divorce, I always feared they would get one. Every night, I would pray as earnestly as a little child could that they would somehow stay together, that somehow they would resolve their differences and save our family.

Even though they both loved my brother and me, the marriage ended. The summer morning when they told us was one of the most painful of my life. My brother and I cried for hours, hoping that our outpouring of emotion would somehow alter the decision. However, it did not. From that day forward, it was as if a cloud had descended on my life, and even years after the divorce, it remained. The fighting that my parents used to do at home only continued over the phone and through lawyers. In the end, it had been a vicious battle that produced no victories and only casualties: my parents, my brother, and me.

DIAGNOSING THE PROBLEM

When I look back at my childhood, I remember very few happy times at home. However, the pain I experienced motivated me to learn from my parents' mistakes. As I grew older and became a Christian, I sought to identify not only what destroyed my parents' relationship, but what afflicts so many relationships that fail. As a result of this careful study and my own experiences, I have come to the following conclusion: broken relationships that produce broken homes are caused by the rejection of God's design for the male/female union. I believe we can avoid this tragedy by adhering to the following three steps:

1) We must stop focusing on *finding* the right mate and begin focusing on *becoming* the right mate. In almost every grocery store, it is difficult to make it through the checkout without seeing magazines that proclaim something to the effect of, "Ten Ways to Find that Perfect Guy." Similarly, during high school and college, most of my friends were fixed on finding that perfect girl. At times, they would even profess to have found her only to learn after a couple of dates that she was not that perfect after all. What I found interesting is that none of them ever said, "You know Bart, it wasn't her. It's me...I'm just not the right one."

Before entering into a relationship with someone else, we should ask, "Am I the man or woman God wants me to be?" While there are many standards to evaluate that question, I always find it wise to return to the Bible. The book of Proverbs contains one of the largest collections of practical guidance in the world, as well as descriptions of what a godly man and woman should be. Proverbs addresses young people several times and in the last chapter, even provides a beautiful depiction of the godly wife. If we focus on fixing ourselves first, we will not only become a better mate, but will be in a better position to one day identify the right mate.

2) We must make sure that when we are finally ready to search for the right person, we are using the right criteria. If a Christian, the Bible says we should only marry other Christians (2 Cor. 6:14). Furthermore, the Bible says we should seek individuals of good character. We put so much importance on characteristics that have no eternal value. Some men are always looking for a beauty that is found only on the cover of an air-brushed magazine; some women are too interested in how much money he may or may not have. Regardless of what meaningless characteristic we focus on, the important thing to remember is that they are all meaningless. While the truth of this might not be evident when dating, it is crystal clear after you have been together several years, have kids, a mortgage payment, and are juggling the other stresses of life. When you have a newborn who is crying, a two-year old who

needs a bath, and two parents who have not slept lately, those concerns—whether it is beauty, money, or anything similar—just do not matter. When you are in the trenches of life, you want someone you can trust—we used to call it in the Army a "battle buddy." If you find a battle buddy of good character, you will navigate life's gauntlet unscathed and with your family intact.

3) We must stop using sex for something it was not intended. One day at college, I was riding the bus to class when I overheard a fellow student exclaim, "My dad would yank me out of this school if he saw this." I stretched my head to see what he was holding. It was the front page of our student newspaper where above the fold there was a large picture of a banana encased in a condom. It was Valentine's Day, and the editors of the paper apparently thought this was an appropriate time to urge students to practice "safe sex." To my shame, I had previously seen the picture earlier in the day and had hardly thought anything about it. But when a fellow student pointed out the absurdity of it, it reminded me that our culture suffers from the delusion that love and sex are the same and the only concern is whether the sex is "safe."

Despite what some believe, the only "safe sex" is that which takes place in the confines of marriage. The God of the universe invented sex and gave us an "Instruction Manual"—the Bible—to govern its proper use. It is as if God one day said, "I love you so much that I've invented this great thing for you to enjoy. But because I love you so much, trust me and listen to what I have to say. Although this gift is wonderful, it is designed for use only within a specific context. If you take it out of that context, it will cease to be a gift. It will be a source of pain for you and others."

Other than reproduction, I believe sex was designed to be the glue that cements the husband and wife union. And yet today, we haphazardly use it as a tool for our enjoyment. Sex has become sport, not too dissimilar from grabbing a quick game of hoops. This is false and counter to what God intends.

The vast majority of single family homes are the result of divorce, the breakup of cohabitating couples, and out-of-wedlock births. If we just used sex in the confines of marriage, we would automatically eliminate the pain caused by the last two—they would cease to exist by definition. By one decision, the pain of so many children could be spared. I also believe similar results could be achieved regarding divorce. If dating couples chose not to have sex before marriage, the relationship would more likely be based on their actual compatibility. Because sex is so powerful, I have noted that it can "paper over" cracks in the relationship. Because sex is so enjoyable, it can make two people really think they love each other when what they really love is having sex together. However, once married, the thrill of sex no longer masks their incompatibility. The cracks in the relationship are exposed and both parties start to say that the other has changed which serves as a useful justification for ending the relationship.

MY STORY

I believe in these steps because they have worked so well in my life. I became a Christian at the age of fifteen. Like most boys that age, my mind was consumed with getting a girl to have an intimate relationship with me. I really did not care about her that much, but I really wanted the physicality, and the more she let me do the more I was interested. However, because I was in the ninth grade and still relatively young, I had yet to find a girl interested in my sexual advances, even though I cloaked them in something more benign.

After becoming a Christian, my views began to change. Although I was aware that the Bible said you should not have sex before marriage, I never understood why. In church, I learned God was not interested in being some sort of cosmic killjoy. He actually wanted me to have the best sex on the planet, but He just wanted me to have it with one person, my wife. It was in church that I learned I should not be lusting over girls in school, that in God's eyes, this was tantamount to having sex with them. Over time, I began to learn God's values which led me to change my own.

As a result of this self-evaluation, I stopped looking for girls and started doing something else. I began to pray the Lord would provide me with a Christian to date and eventually marry. I then began to pray for my future wife, that God would mold her character as He was shaping mine.

A year later, God answered my prayer with a quiet girl by the name of Julie Schulte. That year she actually had taken the bold step of saying she liked me — a real breakthrough for those shy types! I was not sure if I even liked her, but because I knew she was a Christian, I decided to ask her out. One Wednesday afternoon, I borrowed my mom's car and took Julie to an early dinner at McDonald's and then out on our date…to church! I know what you are thinking, this guy is a real Casanova. Apparently Julie thought the same thing, because when I asked her out again, she said she did not like me anymore.

I might not have made a great impression on her, but she made one on me. I never lost interest in that quiet girl who was too shy to look at me. Although I knew other girls who were more popular or maybe more beautiful, there was something about Julie that grabbed my heart. So in my determined fashion, I asked her out again a year later. Unfortunately, I got the same result; she just was not interested. Although dejected and ego bruised, I did not give up. My senior year, I decided to give it one more try, but instead of directly asking her, I talked with some of her friends. They told me she still was not interested.

That seemed like strike three, so I started dating another girl. However, my interest in the other girl grabbed Julie's attention. My relationship with the other girl soon ended, and Julie and I began dating. Starting that senior year of high school, we dated throughout college and finally got married after my first year of law school. On our wedding day, we both said our vows as virgins.

The reason I tell this story is that I think it is worth saying that it can be done. Although Julie and

I cannot claim to have done everything God's way, we did try. We sought to be the right person, then we sought to find the right person, and finally we saved sex for the relationship it was intended—marriage. Although this was difficult, today I thank God for giving us the strength to trust Him. Julie and I have that wonderful, but too uncommon gift, in that we never have to compete with each other's memories of previous loves.

The point is that we can all have this. If you are not the "right one" at the moment, ask God to help you become that person. And when it is time to find the right person, ask God to provide him or her and then make sure your criteria for a mate reflects God's. If you are having sex and are not married, stop. If you have not, keep waiting. For those that might say it is just not worth it, I offer the following challenge. Go ask the happiest married couple you know—call them John and Holly—the following questions: "John, do you wish that Holly had other sexual partners before marrying you?" Or, "Holly, do you think pre-marital sex improves marriages?"

My bet is they will say no to both questions. We must not fail to heed this counsel.

WHAT GOD WANTS FOR YOU

As a child, I remember watching a preacher on television say something that I have never forgotten. I do not know if I was a Christian then or not, but I remember him making the following statement, "The greatest gift a parent can give their child is a great marriage." The preacher went further and said that children even need to see affection between their parents. They need to see them hold one another and feel the love and security of their parents' relationship. As the child of divorce, I automatically saw the truth in these statements. There was no present I wanted more than my parents living happily together.

The relationship between a man and a woman can be such a wonderful experience, but it can also cause unbelievable pain not only to the participants, but also to its innocent products—the children. For that reason, we should do it right. God wants us to experience the greatest love, passion, and devotion available on earth. He wants an interdependence that provides a wonderful security and joy. All God asks is that we do it his way. The inventor of marriage just asks us to follow the instruction book that can be found in most every hotel room—the Bible. We do this, and I believe the words that Sullivan Ballou wrote to Sarah will be more than just an elusive picture of love, but will be our reality.

Chapter 8

What Am I Going to Do with My Life?

For I know the plans I have for you, declares the Lord, plans to prosper you and not to harm you, plans to give you hope and a future.
　　　　　　　　　—Jeremiah 29:11

How is the world going to be different 100 years from now if you achieve your life's mission?
　　　　　　　　　—Dave Ramsey

What am I going to do with my life? We all ask this question. And no matter how old we get or how successful we become, we continue to ask it. We all want to know what path our lives will take and whether it will fulfill our hopes and dreams.

During quiet moments in Iraq, I often pondered this question. I would work out different scenarios in my mind and the consequences of those choices. When time permitted, I ran these ideas by my buddies hoping they might have the answer. Interestingly, the same subject was often on their minds as well. We would exchange ideas and evaluate our plans for the future. But whatever confidence I reached regarding a particular course of action, never lasted. I would always find myself coming back to the question again.

Sitting on my bunk one day, I read something by Dave Ramsey in his book *More Than Enough*. In it he asked the following question, "How is the world going to be different 100 years from now if you achieve your life's mission?" I thought this was a great question because it required self-examination. In a hundred years, I would be dead and with the Father in heaven. My opportunity to make a difference in the world would be gone. From heaven, I would watch eternity unfold and only then see whether my work on earth really mattered — whether it had any eternal consequence.

Walking back from the shower that evening, I began to ask myself the following questions: Does my life really make a difference? Will more people enter the Kingdom of God because of me? Will I really use my gifts and talents to serve God? Will Julie and I raise godly children that will also raise godly children? Will these generations go out in the world and change eternity in the name of Christ?

I returned to my original question—what am I going to do with my life? At that moment, I realized I had been asking the wrong question. The reason I could never get a satisfactory answer was because I had the wrong focus. I was focused on myself. I was focused on what *I* was going to do with *MY* life. Who *I* would become. How much money *I* might earn. Without intending to, I had put myself before God.

From that day forward, I trained myself to ask a different question—How will eternity be different because of me? This question forces me to focus on God. It fixes my mind on God's hopes and dreams, instead of my own. It helps me to see my life in the scope of eternity, instead of the temporal lens of this world. This question helps me orient my life so I may use my limited time on earth to make the greatest impact on eternity.

Once we see our life through this paradigm, we have to put it into practice. In order to do that, I believe we have to recognize two important truths about ourselves.

God Made Us Significant

So many people walk around with a poor self-image. They believe they are no good and that their life consists of nothing more than a meaningless struggle to survive. Over the years, they have been told by parents, teachers, spouses, friends, and colleagues that they just do not count for much. They have heard this so many times that they now believe it. As such, their life is filled with envy, self-doubt, and self-pity.

For many of these folks, they have bought into the greatest lie ever foisted on humankind. The main tenet of this lie is that we are nothing more than a random assortment of atomic elements—our life is simply the product of chance, not creation. Once we buy into this lie, we reason that this life does not matter. And once we come to believe that this life does not matter, we logically have to conclude that neither do we. So then we live a life guided only by what makes us "happy." But after a time, we find that seeking "happiness" never actually makes us very happy. The pursuit does not satisfy; it leaves us empty.

We must rebut this lie and start to see ourselves the way God sees us. The Bible says that God created each of us in his own image (Gen. 1:26). It says that He knew us before our parents knew each other (Psalm 139:16; Jer. 1:5). And finally, it says that when we were in the womb of our mother, He carefully knitted us together (Psalm 139:15).

We are the crowning creation of the God of the universe. In the womb, He crafted us like a great artisan does a painting. And when God looks at us, He sees something far greater than Monet's *Water Lilies* or Van Gogh's *Starry Night*. He sees his masterful creation—a work He cherishes so much that He sacrificed his only Son for it.

It is amazing how young children can sometimes grasp these truths more easily than we can. One of my friends has a daughter named Megan. When

Megan was a little girl, she had severe dyslexia and as a result did not learn to read until the third grade. Before that time, Megan was in Sunday school one morning, and the children were being called on to read from the Bible. When it was Megan's turn, she told the teacher that she could not read. At that time, a little boy turned to her and said, "I guess you're pretty stupid." Megan just smiled, quoted the words of Psalm 139:14, and said, "No, I'm not stupid... the Bible says that I am fearfully and wonderfully made!"

No matter what deformity, disability, or disadvantage we might have, God says that we are fearfully and wonderfully made. We must reprogram our minds with these words. We must tell ourselves over and over—"I am fearfully and wonderfully made." And once we internalize this truth, we must follow little Megan's example and use it as a shield to deflect all the arrows of life.

Our self-worth cannot come from this world. It must come from the living God. And God says to each of us, "You are significant!" If we will only see ourselves through God's eyes, we will become what God intends.

God Has a Plan

On my mother-in-law's refrigerator is a magnet with the following verse: "For I know the plans I have for you, declares the Lord, plans to prosper you and not to harm you, plans to give you hope and a future" (Jer. 29:11). In this short verse, God gives us an incredible insight into his love. Not only did He create us in his divine image, but He also designed a plan for each of our lives. And this is not just any plan; it is a good plan that will bring us hope and a prosperous future.

If God wants us to have a hopeful and prosperous future and we want the same, why do we live lives that are anything but hopeful and prosperous? Why are we so disgruntled and disheartened? Why do we wander around so worried? Why are we missing out on this hopeful and prosperous plan?

I believe that we miss out on God's plan because we insist on living our own. We just do not want to give up control. We believe that through diligent study and hard work we can manage a better alternative. So we plan out our lives without ever really consulting God. At times, we might ask Him to bless our plans, but they are still *OUR* plans. We still want to be in the driver's seat and dictate the path.

But God does not work that way. He will not compete with our egos for lordship, and the idea that we are in control is simply a delusion. The Bible says:

Everything in the heavens and earth is yours, O Lord, and this is your kingdom. We adore you as being in control of everything. Riches and honor come from you alone, and you are the Ruler of all mankind; your hand controls power and might, and it is at your discretion that men are made great and given strength (1 Chron. 29:11-12, TLB).

God is in control of everything. By living our plan, instead of God's, we are simply participating in an exercise of futility. No matter how clever or talented we might be, God is in control, and it is only at his discretion that we will find true success.

Fortunately, God truly wants us to be successful. The Bible says, "In everything you do, put God first, and he will direct you and crown your efforts with success" (Prov. 3:6, TLB). All we have to do is put Him first by prayerfully seeking Him with all our heart (Jer. 29:13). And when we do, God says we will find Him (Jer. 29:14). And in this place of humility, He will reveal his plan for a hopeful and prosperous future.

FOUR HABITS THAT IMPACT ETERNITY

Once we see ourselves through God's eyes and recognize that He has a plan for our future, we are ready for action. In my life, I have come to believe that the following four habits are indispensable for making an eternal impact for God.

Walk with the Wise

It is a principle of life: the company you keep will determine the person you become. The Bible says, "He who walks with the wise grows wise, but the companion of fools suffers harm" (Prov. 13-3). I have seen both sides of this Scripture. I had friends who went to college as one person, but left as someone else. Most of the time, this transformation was a product of the new friends they made. These new friends had different ethical values, which ever so slowly had an impact. As a result, the sober and celibate high school kid became the drunk and promiscuous college student. While it seemed like fun at the time, my friends suffered harm just as the Bible predicts. From alcoholism to venereal disease, they experienced pain and now live with regret. And it all started by becoming the companion of the wrong kind of person.

On the other hand, I have known others who have chosen their companions very carefully. They have purposely sought godly people for employment and friendship, and as a result, have become more godly themselves. I have been blessed to have some very godly friends, one of whom has called me every Sunday night since we graduated from college. For all these years, the only significant interruption of our weekly conversation was my year in Iraq. Throughout these years, I have greatly benefited from his wisdom. He has kept me from suffering harm on numerous occasions and has been an encouragement to my life. Without intending to, I became a wiser man because I spent time with a wise man.

It is for this reason we must choose our companions very carefully. If we are going to make a positive impact on eternity for God, we must associate ourselves with those who have a similar focus. Their wisdom will guide us through the obstacles of life and help us to become all that God desires.

Boldly Answer God's Call

Eric Liddell was a Scottish track star whose life was chronicled in the movie *Chariots of Fire*—the 1981 Academy Award Winner for Best Picture. At the 1924 Olympics in Paris, Liddell was a favorite to win a gold medal in the 100-meter dash. He already held the British record in this distance, a time that would stand for nearly thirty-five years. However, prior to the Olympics, Liddell learned that the 100-meter event was scheduled for a Sunday, and as a committed Christian, he felt he should not run on the Sabbath.

Arriving in Paris, Liddell's stand on faith garnered great attention in the media. And as he lined up to compete in an alternative event—the 400 meters—all eyes were on him. Liddell did not disappoint. In 47.6 seconds, he completed the one lap around the track, some five meters ahead of his nearest competitor. Not only did he win the gold medal, but his time set a new world record. The devout Christian became the hero of the games, and he used this platform to share the gospel with the world.

Following the Olympics, Liddell returned to Scotland, graduated from the University of Edinburgh, and then moved to China to become a missionary. Several years later, World War II began and the Japanese threatened China. The British government urged its nationals to leave the country, but Liddell refused to go. In 1943, the Japanese took over his mission station and placed Liddell in an internment camp, which is where he died two years later. Upon hearing of his death, the entire nation of Scotland mourned.

Too many of us live boring, timid lives. We feel God calling us to act, but because we fear failure, we fail to answer the call. This makes no sense. We do not serve a timid God, and God does not want timid followers. In fact, God calls us to be bold as lions. The Bible says, "The wicked man flees though no one pursues, but the righteous are as bold as a lion" (Prov. 28:1) Eric Liddell knew this, and when he heard God's call, he acted boldly. He stood by his conviction, put his faith in God, and then won a gold medal and set a world record. He then went to China to serve boldly in the mission field, and died in a Japanese internment camp doing the same. If we are to make a positive impact on eternity for God, we must shake our timidity. Whenever we feel the call of God, we must boldly answer the call.

Dismiss the Doubters

Once we feel God's call, we must put in ear plugs. Family, friends, and other well-intentioned people will often try to dissuade us from following the call, especially if the calling is a little unorthodox. Generally, they do this because they care and are worried that we might fail. But if we truly feel the call of God, we must not listen.

David, the future King of Israel, understood this even as a boy. In Judah, the Israelite and Philistine armies faced each other on the battlefield, with the Israelites occupying one hill and the Philistines another. In the valley separating the two, a Philistine giant named Goliath entered every morning and evening to taunt the Israelites. Goliath dared any Israelite to fight him, but upon hearing his words, they only fled in fear.

This changed when David arrived. Hearing Goliath's challenge, David became overcome with righteous outrage. He asked, "Who is this uncircumcised Philistine that he should defy the armies of the living God?" (1 Sam. 17:26). He then went to Saul, the Israelite King, and told him that he would fight Goliath. But instead of thanking David, Saul discouraged him saying, "You are not able to go out against this Philistine and fight him; you are only a boy, and he has been a fighting man from his youth" (1 Sam. 17:33).

It is easy to miss the significance of this statement. David was just a young shepherd boy, and here was his King telling him he could not win. It is hard to imagine a more discouraging word spoken by a more prominent person. It would be like the president of the United States coming to me and saying, "Bart, you just don't have what it takes to win...you need to give up!" This would cause me to pause. But not David, he refused to waver. He felt the calling of God and dismissed his powerful doubting King. He replied to Saul with the following:

Your servant has been keeping his father's sheep. When a lion or a bear came and carried off a sheep from the flock, I went after it, struck it and rescued the sheep from its mouth.

When it turned on me, I seized it by its hair, struck it and killed it. Your servant has killed both the lion and the bear; this uncircumcised Philistine will be like one of them, because he has defied the armies of the living God. The Lord who delivered me from the paw of the lion and the paw of the bear will deliver me from the hand of this Philistine (1 Sam. 17:34-37).

And that is exactly what happened. With only a sling and a stone, David brought down the mighty giant.

I have faced similar tests of faith several times in my life. I have heard the call of God, but then wavered after listening to those who doubted the wisdom of my plan. Most recently, I faced this when deciding whether to write this book. When I left Iraq, I was absolutely convinced that I should write it. However, once I got home and began to share my idea with others, they expressed concern. They worried how I would support my growing family while taking time off from work to write. Others questioned whether this was a good idea seeing that I was not an accomplished writer. Some just wondered whether this was the best use of my talents.

One day while struggling with self-doubt, the Lord came to my aid. His messenger was my brother, Brett. I told him about my worries: lack of money, new baby on the way, and limited writing ability. Given all of these issues, I said that I was questioning whether it made sense for me to take on such a project. Brett paused and then simply asked, "Do you really feel that God is calling you to write this book?" I thought for a second, took a deep breath, and said, "Well...yes." He then replied, "Bart, if you really feel that God is calling you to write this book, then you have no choice...you must write it."

I knew he was right. Whenever God calls, we must respond. He is our Father and Lord, and nothing worth having can be found outside his will. After my brother's words, something changed inside of me. My spine seemed to straighten and my resolve stiffened. I began to fully embrace the call of God, and as a result, my worries and those of others no longer mattered. I still did not know how I would manage to write the book, but I decided I would trust Him and answer the call. And when other doubters came forward, I just smiled, but did not hesitate. My mind was fixed; I was going to answer the call. It is a principle: to make an eternal impact for God, we must dismiss the doubters.

Say, "I can."

The Bible says, "I can do all things through Christ who strengthens me" (Phil. 4:13, NKJV). Few have understood this better than George Washington Carver. Born into slavery during the Civil War, Carver went on to become one of the most prominent men of the twentieth century. He did not learn to read or write until age twenty. But because he wanted an education, he managed to work his way through high school and college, eventually earning a bachelor's and master's degree in agriculture.[1] Following graduation, Carver joined the faculty of the Tuskegee Institute (now Tuskegee University) which was an agricultural and industrial school for black Americans.

At Tuskegee, Carver became the leading agricultural scientist of his generation. He discovered hundreds of products for little used crops like the peanut and sweet potato. As he had hoped, these products helped the poor farmer—both black and white alike—survive the boll-weevil invasion which ravaged Southern cotton. For his work on the peanut, Carver was asked to testify before Congress in 1921. His presentation was so insightful that Congress had him speak for almost two hours, instead of the customary ten minutes. This gesture would have been uncommon for any Congressional witness, but unheard of for a black man.

Despite fame and notoriety, Carver refused to capitalize on opportunities for wealth. He would not accept payment for his agricultural innovations and shortly before his death, gave Tuskegee his life savings ($33,000) to establish a foundation for research in chemistry.[2] He remained at Tuskegee until he died in 1943. That same year Congress dedicated a national monument in Carver's name near Diamond, Missouri. Not only was this the first national monument dedicated to a black American, but also the first to a non-president.

What few know about Carver is that he was a man of faith. He often referred to God as "Mr. Creator" and taught a Bible class to the Tuskegee students on

Sundays.[3] Carver once wrote, "I want [my students] to find Jesus...How I long for each one to walk and talk with the Great Creator through the things He has created."[4] Carver knew that he could do all things through Christ who strengthened him. God had shown him that time and time again.

When I graduated from law school, my cousin sent me a poem by Edgar A. Guest titled *Equipment*. This was Carver's favorite poem, and he read it to each of his classes so that they might understand that God equipped them with everything they needed to succeed. Because we need to learn the same, I include it below.

EQUIPMENT

Figure it out for yourself, my lad,
You've all that the greatest of men have had,
Two arms, two hands, two legs, two eyes
And a brain to use if you would be wise.
With this equipment they all began,
So start for the top and say, "I can."

Look them over, the wise and great
They take their food from a common plate,
And similar knives and forks they use,
With similar laces they tie their shoes.
The world considers them brave and smart,
But you've all they had when they made their start.

You can triumph and come to skill,
You can be great if you only will.
You're well equipped for what fight you choose,
You have legs and arms and a brain to use,
And the man who has risen great deeds to do
Began his life with no more than you.

You are the handicap you must face,
You are the one who must choose your place,
You must say where you want to go,
How much you will study the truth to know.
God has equipped you for life, but He
Lets you decide what you want to be.

Courage must come from the soul within,
The man must furnish the will to win.
So figure it out for yourself, my lad.
You were born with all that the great have had,
With your equipment they all began,
Get hold of yourself and say: "I can."

God wants to do amazing things through our lives. Even if we feel inadequate, God gave us everything we need to do all that He wants—we are endowed with all the equipment necessary to succeed. Our only challenge is to trust Him. Decide today to make an eternal impact for God because nothing else matters. All we have to do is follow the advice of a former slave and say, I can!

Chapter 9

Your Father's Greatest Hope

For God so loved the world that He gave His only begotten Son, that whoever believes in Him should not perish but have everlasting life.

—John 3:16 (NKJV)

There is a God-shaped vacuum in the heart of every person and it can never be filled by any created thing. It can only be filled by God, made known through Jesus Christ.

—Blaise Pascal

About two thousand years ago, the Bible says that a man named Jesus walked the earth. Regardless of whom you might believe Him to be, it is without dispute that his words and actions sparked an incredible movement. From one small town this movement spread across the entire globe. Now, over one billion people claim to follow Him. His birth is the basis for the world's dating system and the most celebrated holiday. The book that describes his life is the most popular one ever printed. It is undeniable; Jesus was a man that made an impact.

Like all influential people in history, we ask, "Who was He?" Well, the Bible says that Jesus claimed to be the Christ, the Son of God (Matt. 26:63-67). He claimed the authority to forgive sins—as if He were the offended party (Mark 2:5-12)—and even claimed to be the only gateway to God, saying that no one could come before the Father except through Him (John 14:6). Of course, if someone made such statements today, we would dismiss him immediately. However, because of Jesus' undeniable impact on the world, we cannot simply dismiss Him or sidestep his deity by calling Him a great moral teacher. Regardless of our background or religious persuasion, we are forced to deal with what He said about himself. Logic compels us to determine if this man is who He claimed to be.

Interestingly, it was during World War II and the bombings of Britain when C.S. Lewis was asked to do the same thing. Lewis is mostly remembered today as a professor (Oxford and Cambridge) and author of more than thirty books including the popular children stories, *The Chronicles of Narnia*. What is much less known about C.S. Lewis is that he was a veteran of the trenches of World War I—a war so horrific that it was considered "the war to end all wars." However, just twenty-four years later, Hitler forced Great Britain to war again, and its ordinary citizens served on the front lines as four hundred planes bombarded their cities every night. At a time when the British people faced fear and constant death, the BBC invited Lewis—a former atheist himself—to give a series of radio lectures addressing the central tenets of Christianity. The contents of these lectures to a war-torn people were later converted to text and published as *Mere Christianity*.

It is in this book that one finds arguably the most famous argument for the deity of Christ. Lewis writes:

> I am trying here to prevent anyone saying the really foolish thing that people often say about Him: 'I'm ready to accept Jesus as a great moral teacher, but I don't accept His claim to be God.' That is the one thing we must not say. A man who was merely a man and said the sort of things Jesus said would not be a great moral teacher. He would either be a lunatic—on a level with the man who says he is a poached egg—or else he would be the Devil of Hell. You must make your choice. Either this man was, and is, the Son of God: or else a madman or something worse. You can shut Him up for a fool, you can spit at Him and kill Him as a demon; or you can fall at His feet and call Him Lord and God. But let us not come with any patronizing nonsense about His being a great human teacher. He has not left that open to us. He did not intend to.[1]

A SAVIOR

In my own life, I have come to conclude that not only did a man named Jesus walk the earth, but that the New Testament accurately reflects what He said and did.[2] I have faced C.S. Lewis' challenge, and am convinced that Jesus is neither a liar nor lunatic, but is in fact the Lord. However, when I began my relationship with Christ, I did it without the benefit of C.S. Lewis' arguments or the other defenses of the Christian faith. I simply heard the gospel message, and like Paul on the road to Damascus, knew I was hearing from God.

I was fifteen, and my good friend Robert took me to a "lock-in" with his church's youth group. The term "lock-in" refers to the fact that we were actually locked inside the church overnight. Being that we were a bunch of teenagers, we certainly did not sleep. Instead, we ate snacks, played sports in the gym, and basically had a good time all night long.

Sometime during the night, the youth minister brought us together to share a message from the Bible. While I was not a "church-goer," I still prayed every night before bed. Even if I did not know that much about God, I certainly believed He was there.

And while I do not remember everything the youth pastor said that night, his words struck a chord in my heart. He said that the God of the universe wanted to be my Savior. That through Jesus, God wanted to have a personal relationship with me. All I had to do was to invite Him into my life.

Somehow, I had a moment of clarity. It was as if a thousand-piece jigsaw puzzle were randomly spread out before me. And then quickly, God assembled it together before my eyes, leaving only the final, center piece. He then hands it to me. Looking at the piece and the puzzle with the missing hole, I know that it fits—I know it makes sense—I know it completes the picture.

In the back of the gym that night, I decided to finish the puzzle. With the help of someone from the church, I prayed the following prayer:

> Lord Jesus, I need you. Thank you for dying on the cross for my sins. I ask you to come into my heart as my Savior and Lord. Take control of my life and help me be the kind of person you want me to be. Amen.

NOT JUST A SAVIOR, A DADDY

With that simple prayer, Jesus Christ became my personal Savior. To my surprise, I would later learn that I also became his adopted son. The Bible says, "For he chose us in him before the creation of the world to be holy and blameless in his sight. In love he predestined us to be adopted as his sons through Jesus Christ, in accordance with his pleasure and will—to the praise of his glorious grace, which he has freely given us in the One he loves" (Eph. 1:4-6).

This statement is such a powerful expression of the Father's love. Even after being a Christian all these years, hypocrisy and self-centeredness still better characterize my life more than any other virtue. I am a grown man who knows better, not a cute, innocent child. Better than anyone, God knows this. Yet, through his Son Jesus, the God of the universe still looks at me—and everyone like me—and says, "I want you...I want to adopt you as my son."

To really grasp how unique this is, just briefly picture the face of the most terrible villain in human history. Now picture the most virtuous man in your home town. For a second, imagine if this virtuous man were to one day announce, with the villain's consent, that he is going to file the paperwork to adopt the villain. If you were a friend, you would probably try to intervene. Even if you were just an acquaintance, you might petition the court to have him declared insane. In our thinking, this just does not make sense. But to God, thankfully it does.

The love that a devoted father has for his child is difficult to explain. Yet in just a few lines, Jesus tells what is in my opinion, one of the most powerful father/child stories committed to paper.

Jesus continued: "There was a man who had two sons. The younger one said to his father, 'Father, give me my share of the estate.' So he divided his property between them.

"Not long after that, the younger son got together all he had, set off for a distant country and there squandered his wealth in wild living. After he had spent everything, there was a severe famine in that whole country, and he began to be in need. So he went and hired himself out to a citizen of that country, who sent him to his fields to feed pigs. He longed to fill his stomach with the pods that the pigs were eating, but no one gave him anything.

"When he came to his senses, he said, 'How many of my father's hired men have food to spare, and here I am starving to death! I will set out and go back to my father and say to him: Father, I have sinned against heaven and against you. I am no longer worthy to be called your son; make me like one of your hired men.' So he got up and went to his father.

"But while he was still a long way off, his father saw him and was filled with compassion for him; he ran to his son, threw his arms around him and kissed him.

"The son said to him, 'Father, I have sinned against heaven and against you. I am no longer worthy to be called your son.'

"But the father said to his servants, 'Quick! Bring the best robe and put it on him. Put a ring on his finger and sandals on his feet. Bring the fattened calf and kill it. Let's have a feast and celebrate. For this son of mine was dead and is alive again; he was lost and is found.' (Luke 15:11-24).

I believe that each of us is this prodigal son. We have all chosen not to follow the Father's will for our lives and tried to do things our own way. The amazing thing is that God never gives up on us. Like any loving daddy, He sits on the front porch just waiting for us to come home. And when we do, no matter how awfully we behaved when away, He asks no questions. He just runs to us and greets us with a big hug and a kiss. He puts a ring on our finger, sandals on our feet, and celebrates.

Instead of an austere father, I believe God wants us to see Him as a daddy. In fact, the Bible says that God's spirit within us cries out "Abba, Father" (Gal. 4:6). In Aramaic, "Abba" basically means Daddy, and I believe God desires the tender relationship that only the word "Daddy" connotes. And like the prodigal son, it is my hope that we will run home to Him. That through Jesus, we will seek a relationship with our Father in heaven and that in Him we will see a daddy that loves us.

To my children, as your daddy, I ask that you embrace your Daddy in heaven as you would embrace me. It is the most important decision you will make and my greatest desire for your life. When you do, I believe legions of angels will rejoice, and if I am gone, I will celebrate in heaven with them.

Notes

Chapter 1: War's Greatest Gift

1. Stu Weber, *Tender Warrior* (Sisters, OR: Multnomah Publishers, 1999), 16.
2. Ibid.

Chapter 2: Character Under Fire

1. Josh White and Bradley Graham, "Military Says It Paid Iraq Papers for News," *The Washington Post* (3 December 2005).
2. Ibid.
3. Josh White and Jonathan Finer, "Senator Seeks Answers on Iraq Stories," *The Washington Post* (2 December 2005).
4. Josh White and Bradley Graham, "Military Says It Paid Iraq Papers for News," *The Washington Post* (3 December 2005).
5. Mark Mazzetti and David S. Cloud, "Pentagon Audit Clears Propaganda Effort," *The New York Times* (20 October 2006).

6. C.S. Lewis, *Mere Christianity* (San Francisco, CA: Harper Collins, 2001), 8.

7. Ibid., 5.

8. Stephen E. Ambrose, *Band of Brothers* (New York, NY: Simon & Schuster, 1992), 179.

9. Ibid., 189.

10. Stephen R. Covey, *The 7 Habits of Highly Effective People* (New York, NY: Simon & Schuster, 1989), 196.

11. Andy Stanley, *Like a Rock: Becoming a Person of Character* (Nashville, TN: Thomas Nelson Publishers, 1997), 30-31.

12. Army Field Manual 6-22, *Army Leadership— Competent, Confident, and Agile* (Washington D.C.: Headquarters, Department of the Army, 12 October 2006), para 7-54.

13. Editor Keith E. Puls, *Law of War Handbook* (Charlottesville, VA: The Judge Advocate General's Legal Center and School, 2004), 117-119.

Chapter 3: Six Signs of the Faithful Follower

1. Andy Stanley [Audio CD] *Taking Care of Business: Part 1 — Meet the Boss* (Alpharetta, GA: North Point Ministries: 2002).

Chapter 4: Five Facets of the Lasting Leader

1. Army Field Manual 6-22, *Army Leadership— Competent, Confident, and Agile* (Washington D.C.: Headquarters, Department of the Army, 12 October 2006), para 1-2.

2. Michael Shaara, *The Killer Angels* (New York, NY: Ballantine Books, 1974), 26.
3. General George S. Patton Jr., *War As I Knew It* (1947).
4. Marine Corps Doctrinal Publication 1, *Warfighting* (Washington D.C.: Headquarters, United States Marine Corps, 20 June 1997), 86.
5. Dwight D. Eisenhower Library, Pre-Presidential Papers, Principal File: Butcher Diary 1942-1945, ARC Identifier: 186470.

Chapter 5: Fit for the Fight

1. Army Field Manual 6-22, *Army Leadership—Competent, Confident, and Agile* (Washington D.C.: Headquarters, Department of the Army, 12 October 2006), para.5-9.
2. Peter Collier with David Horowitz, *The Roosevelts: An American Saga* (New York, NY: Simon & Schuster, 1994), 100.
3. Ibid., 168.
4. Ibid., 242.
5. Ibid., 39-40.

Chapter 6: Financially Free

1. "Personal savings drop to a 73-year low," *The Associated Press* (1 February 2007).
2. The Washington Times Editorial Board, "Debt and the Bush budgets," *The Washington Times* (13 February 2007).

3. Robert Rector, *How "Poor" are America's Poor?*, Background #791 Heritage Foundation.

4. Howard Dayton, *Your Money Counts* (Wheaton, IL: Tyndale House Publishers, 1996), 46-47.

5. Ibid., 8.

6. Ron Blue, *Master Your Money* (Chicago, IL: Moody Publishers, 2004), 132-133.

7. Thomas J. Stanley and William D. Danko, *The Millionaire Next Door* (New York, NY: Pocket Books, 1996), 112-113.

Chapter 7: Making Marriage Matter

1. Evan C. Jones, "Sullivan Ballou: The Macabre Fate of a American Civil War Major" *America's Civil War* magazine, November 2004. Retrieved 7 March 2007, from http://www.historynet.com/wars_conflicts/american_civil_war/3033061.html?page=1&c=y.

2. This statement does not account for those who God has called to be single. As the apostle Paul makes clear, God has given some this gift.

3. Sam Roberts, "It's Official: To Be Married Means to Be Outnumbered," *New York Times* (15 October 2006).

4. Ibid.

5. David Popenoe and Barbara Dafoe Whitehead, "Marriage and Family: What Does the Scandinavian Experience Tell Us?" (The National Marriage Project, The State

University of Rutgers, 2005), 8. Retrieved 7 March 2007, from http://marriage.rutgers. edu/Publications/SOOU/TEXTSOOU2005. htm.

6. Sam Roberts, "It's Official: To Be Married Means to Be Outnumbered," *New York Times* (15 October 2006).

7. Sharon Jayson, "Divorce declining, but so is marriage," *USA TODAY* (18 July 2005).

8. Sam Roberts, "It's Official: To Be Married Means to Be Outnumbered," *New York Times* (15 October 2006).

9. Sarah McLanahan and Gary Sandefur, *Growing Up With a Single Parent: What Hurts, What Helps* (Cambridge, MA: Harvard University Press, 1996), 2-3.

10. Ibid., 1.

Chapter 8: What Am I Going to Do with My Life?

1. "Dr. Carver is Dead; Negro Scientist," *New York Times* (6 January 1943).

2. Ibid.

3. Ibid.

4. In Touch Ministries, "Why Did You Make The Peanut?" Retrieved March 7, 2007, from www.intouch.org/myintouch/mighty/ portraits/george_washington_carver_ 213625.html.

Chapter 9: Your Father's Greatest Hope

1. C.S. Lewis, *Mere Christianity* (San Francisco, CA: Harper Collins, 2001), 52.

2. See, *The Case for Christ* by Lee Strobel; *Why I Believe* by D. James Kennedy: and *More Than A Carpenter* by Josh McDowell.

I Want to Hear from You!

W riting this book has been a challenging but rewarding experience for me and my family. I pray that the words God put on my heart have enriched your life. If you have any questions or comments about this book or for me personally, I want to hear from you. Please email me at the following address: info@bartnewman.com.

Thank you for taking the time to read this book and may God lead you as you strive to get the most out of this life!

LaVergne, TN USA
30 September 2009
159534LV00001B/4/P